"Is traditional marketing definitely dead? For most observers in the marketing and communications fields, it is less and less efficient, and consumers are more and more resistant to its methods. In this context, 'implicative marketing' is a breakthrough: it allows students and professionals to imagine new ways of promoting products and services, based on peer-to-peer principles instead of top-down communications. A precious contribution by Florence Touzé."

*Hervé Monier, brandnewsblog.com*

"This book invents a new and more responsible mission for marketing. Based on a critical analysis of the current role of marketing in the vast majority of companies, it describes emerging practices and makes concrete suggestions for a marketing that contributes to a positive social and environmental impact."

*André Sobczak, Associate Dean of Faculty and Research,*
*Audencia Business School*

# Implicative Marketing

This book is a manifesto for responsible marketing. Taking a critical look at marketing practices of the last 50 years, it explains why they have led to an ethical stalemate and sometimes even a business impasse.

Exposed to such practices, consumers have grown tired of meaningless offers coupled with the destruction of value as prices are driven down. As a result, today's marketing professionals find themselves in the firing line of a combat focused on greater social responsibility and environmental sustainability. Thanks to new ways of understanding consumers and branding, this book suggests how such a challenge can be met. Through the presentation of experiences, studies and concrete cases, the reader gains a tangible, fresh perspective on marketing: a new global, responsible, creative and collaborative model that helps respect sustainable consumption.

*Implicative Marketing* presents a paradigm shift, one that will be of considerable interest not just to academics and their students, but also to marketing practitioners.

**Florence Touzé** is Professor and Head of Brand Communication Studies at Audencia Business School, France, and holder of the Chair in Corporate Social Responsibility and Responsible Branding.

# Routledge Focus on Business and Management

The fields of business and management have grown exponentially as areas of research and education. This growth presents challenges for readers trying to keep up with the latest important insights. Routledge Focus on Business and Management presents small books on big topics and how they intersect with the world of business research.

Individually, each title in the series provides coverage of a key academic topic, whilst collectively, the series forms a comprehensive collection across the business disciplines.

**Employment Relations and Ethnic Minority Enterprise**
An Ethnography of Chinese Restaurants in the UK
*Xisi Li*

**Women, Work and Migration**
Nursing in Australia
*Diane van den Broek and Dimitria Groutsis*

**Distributed Leadership and Digital Innovation**
The Argument for Couple Leadership
*Caterina Maniscalco*

**Public Relations Crisis Communication**
A New Model
*Lisa Anderson-Meli and Swapna Koshy*

**Implicative Marketing**
For a Sustainable Economy
*Florence Touzé*

For more information about this series, please visit: www.routledge.com/ Routledge-Focus-on-Business-and-Management/book-series/FBM

# Implicative Marketing

For a Sustainable Economy

**Florence Touzé**

LONDON AND NEW YORK

First published 2020
by Routledge
2 Park Square, Milton Park, Abingdon, Oxon OX14 4RN

and by Routledge
52 Vanderbilt Avenue, New York, NY 10017

*Routledge is an imprint of the Taylor & Francis Group, an informa business*

*British Library Cataloguing-in-Publication Data*
A catalogue record for this book is available from the British Library

*Library of Congress Cataloging-in-Publication Data*
Names: Touzé, Florence, author.
Title: Implicative marketing : for a sustainable economy / Florence Touzé.
Description: Abingdon, Oxon ; New York, NY : Routledge, 2020. |
Series: Routledge focus on business and management | Includes
bibliographical references and index.
Identifiers: LCCN 2020003486 (print) | LCCN 2020003487 (ebook)
Subjects: LCSH: Marketing–Moral and ethical aspects. |
Sustainable development. | Industrial management. | Branding
(Marketing) Classification: LCC HF5415 .T68 2020 (print) |
LCC HF5415 (ebook) | DDC 658.8–dc23
LC record available at https://lccn.loc.gov/2020003486
LC ebook record available at https://lccn.loc.gov/2020003487

ISBN: 978-0-367-44556-0 (hbk)
ISBN: 978-1-003-01034-0 (ebk)

Typeset in Times New Roman
by Wearset Ltd, Boldon, Tyne and Wear

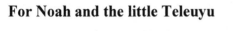

For Noah and the little Teleuyu

# Contents

# Figures

# Tables

# About the author

Florence Touzé is a professor at the Audencia Business School,[1] where she holds the chair in corporate social responsibility. She is also director of brand advertising programs at Audencia Business School (Audencia SciencesCom).

After a career at an advertising consulting agency, Florence Touzé offered her expertise in consumer behaviour and advertising in higher education. She teaches courses and conducts research on the history of marketing and on how the brand concept is becoming increasingly associated with greater corporate responsibility. In particular, her work involves persuading corporations to produce sustainable merchandise, regain consumer trust, and change their advertising to express sincere commitment, respectfully but effectively.

Florence Touzé is an active participant in the public debate on responsible advertising and the marketing sector in France. Specifically, she is a partner of the Succeed with Responsible Marketing platform and a member of the examining commission for the Grand Prize for Marketing Excellence at Adetem. She lectures on these subjects to corporations and professional associations.

According to Touzé,

> Since the 2000s, instead of presenting sustainable development and advertising as opposites of each other, I wanted to question their concepts and practices: how can we place advertising and marketing at the service of the transition? Today, the issue of brand responsibility is the core of my efforts. And almost 20 years later, there is still a lot of work to be done!

## Note

1 See https://faculte-recherche.audencia.com/cvs/cv/florence-touze/?no_cache=1& cHash=8ac82b9ffea6080c05546abea11a1833

# Foreword

It is my pleasure to introduce Florence Touzé's controversial yet optimistic contribution to the ongoing and vitally important discussions occurring in marketing and management. *Implicative Marketing* is an interesting and accessible text that critically examines the marketing practices of the last 50 years. It does this in order to help the reader understand how marketers have contributed to the ethical stalemate that marketing now faces. Touzé argues that this stalemate is a consequence of the fact that consumers have been inundated with offers that have undermined value by driving prices down. In so doing, marketers have helped foster unsustainable levels of consumption and encouraged a general disregard for the broader long-term social and environmental good.

Informed by this analysis, Touzé then presents a perspective that, if accepted, will ensure that advertising and marketing and the organizations these functions serve are participants in the transition to a more positive and sustainable future. She presents a clear and realistic proposal for how to integrate advertising and marketing into this transition, a proposal that requires marketers to accept the legitimacy of the urgent calls for change from opinion leaders across the globe and choose to become a voice for fairer access to, and sustainable use of, the World's resources. In simple terms, she is inviting marketers to become key players in creating a new economic model that will stem irresponsible organizational practices that have led to inequitable and unsustainable levels of consumption and caused social and environmental harm on a global scale.

Like many other commentators, she considers that marketers have been deeply implicated, if not complicit,[1] in economic policy making and commercial decisions that have led to the current environmental and social distress facing the planet and its people. However, it is not her intention to participate in the "blame game". She moves beyond this to propose that, just as marketers have contributed to high consumption life styles, presented dubious product claims, and supported wasteful use of resources, they can and should become full partners in creating a more sustainable pathway forward. She is one of the many contemporary marketing scholars who believe marketing, when harnessed responsibly, can be a vital force in changing behaviour in ways that will inch humanity closer to a socially equitable and environmentally sustainable future. After all, not only have marketers supported the emergence of the prevailing capitalist economic model by successfully encouraging consumers to recalibrate their beliefs about the virtues, as opposed to the vices, of consumption,[2] increasing numbers of marketers are now using the same techniques they employed to encourage unsustainable levels of consumption to advocate for more sustainable consumer behaviours, such as product reuse, repurposing and recycling, and the rejection of unnecessary packaging.[3]

Already there is evidence in the literatures of the now well-established fields of green, sustainable, and social marketing that confirms there is a will among many marketers to contribute to the transition to better ways of managing resources, distributing power in the marketplace, and sustainably satisfying social, economic, and environmental needs. Some would say that the pioneering scholarship in these fields contains all the ingredients necessary to bring about the required transition.[4] However, the quantum of change required to transform consumer behaviour and avert the widely predicted environmental and social catastrophes continues to prove difficult to achieve despite the weight of argument supporting the need for this transformation to happen.[5] Part of the problem appears to be that it is not entirely clear what sustainability would be like in practice. This is linked to the fact that sustainability has been variously defined and even questioned as a realistic goal. Possibly the most popular view is captured in the definition offered by Fodness[6] who defines sustainability in line with the OECD's (2002)[7] definition, as "meeting the needs of the present without compromising the ability of future generations to meet their own needs" (p. 10). Touze's notion of *Implicative Marketing* moves beyond this increasingly mainstream understanding of sustainability and the green and socially responsible practices it has helped to foster in industry and commerce. She argues that in marketing a new, more tangible, perspective is needed if the fundamental changes in economic thinking and consumer behaviour required to bring the World back from the edge of catastrophic disaster are to occur.

*Implicative Marketing* proposes a marketing paradigm shift that moves the reader beyond the familiar notions of sustainable practice and social responsibility, which are increasingly being used to justify changes in consumer behaviour. Directing this shift is her assertion that only when marketers accept that they are implicated in the outcomes of the brand development and consumption they advocate can they be fully-fledged participants in the transition to a socially responsible and environmentally sustainable World. She uses an array of powerful examples to expose the destructive nature of traditional approaches to marketing in order to justify an alternative sustainable marketing approach that allows the marketer to act upon this assertion. The result, she claims, will be a positive and constructive form of marketing that will become a resource for companies as they reframe their purpose and step forward as socially responsible and environmentally sustainable actors in the urgent quest to save the planet.

Touzé is realistic. She recognizes that the challenges are considerable and marketers are only one of many groups whose policies and practices combine to enact an economic system. At the same time, she is convinced that marketers are ideally equipped to have significant agency in instituting a new economic order. She is proposing that the extent of this agency will be determined by the degree to which marketers accept that they are inextricably implicated in the social and environmental consequences of the consumption they promote. Only when they accept personal responsibility will marketing will be able to apply its considerable influence effectively and be a key force in the process of ushering in constructive change.

It is this proposition that marketers and the organizations they serve should be responsible for the consequences of the actions they promote to others that is the key to understanding and acting upon Touzé's message. If marketers accept that they are not simply connected to the social and economic consequences of their marketing practice but personally complicit, and so have co-responsibility for them, then marketing and marketing education will undergo a comprehensive transformation. This will require critically reflecting on, and in many cases renovating, core values, mission statements, guidelines for professional practice, codes of conduct and institutional logics. Thus, Touzé is not simply suggesting a semantic change.

In conclusion, *Implicative Marketing* is a mandate for a radical change in the *raison d'être* and the *modus operandi* of marketing as a discipline, profession and management process. I think you will agree that Florence Touzé has produced a highly persuasive text that encourages the reader to think differently about marketing and its potential to contribute to a better future.

Colleen E. Mills PhD
Professor of Management
University of Canterbury Business School
Christchurch, NEW ZEALAND
colleen.mills@canterbury.ac.nz

# Notes

1 De Graaf *et al.* (2005); James (2007).
2 de la Vega (March, April, May 2011).
3 Gordon, Carrigan, and Hastings (2011).
4 Gordon, Carrigan, and Hastings, 2011.
5 Strengers and Maller (2015).
6 Fodness (2015).
7 OECD (2002).

# References

De Graaf, J., Wann, D., and Naylor, T.H. (2005). *Affluenza: The All-consuming Epidemic* (2nd edn). San Francisco, CA: Berrett-Koehler.

de la Vega, X. (March, April, May 2011). Consommer: Comment la consommation a envahi nos vies. *Sciences Humaines, Grands Dossiers*, 22. www.sciences humaines.com/consommer-comment-la-consommation-a-envahi-nos-vies_fr_398.htm.

Fodness, D. (2015). Managing the wickedness of socially responsible marketing, *Journal of Business Strategy*, 36(5), 10–17.

Gordon, R., Carrigan, M., and Hastings, G. (2011). A framework for sustainable marketing. *Marketing Theory*, *11*(2), 143–163.

James, O. (2007). *Affluenza.* London: Vermilion.

OECD (2002). *Towards sustainable household consumption? Trends and policies in OECD countries.*

Strengers, Y. and Maller, C. (2015). Social practices, interventions and sustainability: Beyond behavioural change. In Strengers, Y. and Maller, C. (eds), *Social Practices, Interventions and Sustainability: Beyond Behaviour Change* (pp. 1–12). London: Routledge.

# Preface

This book is for everyone interested in marketing and advertising.

It is also for everyone who criticizes marketers and advertising and for everyone who practices in these professions.

And, of course, for my students.

This book is not a manual.

It is not a lesson.

It is not a book on sustainable development.

It is not pro- or anti-marketing.

It is a point of view, a line of thought.

It is the outcome of years of observation, reports on anomalies, and the discovery of elegant ideas.

It has been a source of annoyance and real anger sometimes.

And enthusiasm, desires, and hopes.

In short, it is a personal and sincere testimony and a proposal that I hope will create dialogue, debate, and personal bonds.

*Florence Touzé*

# Acknowledgements

Many thanks
To those who helped me,

- **Colleen Mills**, for her unfailing support and assistance
- **Sandrine** and **Yannick Roudaut** from *La mer salée*, for their convictions, their enthusiasm and their trust.

**To the people who inspired me:**

- My students at Audencia,
- The CSR chair team at Audencia, namely, Mélanie Dugué, Anne-Laure Guiheneuf, and André Sobczak,
- The entire "Succeed with responsible marketing" team (see www. reussir-avec-un-marketing-responsable.org/).

And, most of all, many thanks to my family for everything you did for me.

# Introduction

Why do journalists and other media commentators like to use the term marketing with a negative connotation? Why are many of the commercial or political promotions in the public arena that do not achieve the desired effect derided as marketing or mere advertising?

How did these two management terms – marketing and advertising – become dirty words, synonyms for trickery, for superficiality, for the contemptible, even for swindle or deceit, and, at the very least, spin? Is it because those words were overused? There is no doubt about it. Perhaps it is because journalists scorn trade? Perhaps. Or is it because the antics of those marketing and advertising have been so excessive (and conducted at the consumer's expense) that their legitimacy has been forfeited? This is the core issue of concern.

We also have to question those they serve. Why does Apple make us buy a new charger every time we buy a new computer? Why do school satchels for September arrive on supermarket shelves on July 1? Why does a child's t-shirt made at the other end of the planet sell for less than a pack of yogurt? And after three, four, and five blades, will razors shave better if they have six blades? And, tomorrow, will there be seven or eight?

Today's marketing, which supports such actions, is nothing but a bag of tricks whose mystery dissipated long ago. True, marketing can still create cravings and sell billions of dollars' worth of products but its bogus promises have become so outrageously misleading that it has lost all credibility. It has overturned price benchmarks, hastened obsolescence, and even had the audacity to resort to greenwashing. Marketing's headlong rush to encourage consumption in any way possible has turned off even the most addicted consumer.

Consumers are increasingly experiencing cognitive dissonance: the headlines scream about global food waste while the same sources participate in advertising campaigns for pay-what-you-want restaurants and food banks. When discussing palm oil, which aspect is more distressing, the apparent harm to our health or the environmental disaster it causes? Zara and Levi's constantly offer us new ways of looking trendy, but due to a negative publicity campaign orchestrated by Greenpeace,[1] both brands were forced to acknowledge publicly how harmful their wares really are. And we can add to this list Volkswagen's Dieselgate, the devastation industrial fishing fleets wreak on sea life, and the Rana Plaza collapse.[2]

As everyday individuals, how can we take in all such disparate messages on a daily basis without questioning our own consumption? How long will this go on? And how should we comprehend this omnipresent and paradoxical collection of practices we call marketing?

By focusing on the desires that it has created itself, marketing has become insane. It has forgotten about limits on resources, waste, the permanent pollution of entire regions, and evidence of the planet's escalating inability to absorb more waste. It has forgotten about obesity, social injustice, and the lack of transparency of global supply chains. It has also forgotten to pay attention to consumers' deepest yearnings and to respect wage earners. Last, it has forgotten to enquire into the existential doubt that individuals experience in an era of planetary convulsions that suddenly makes the satisfaction of essential material needs seem precarious. It has denied the widespread awareness of the harm wrought by overconsumption.

Is marketing in the process of forgetting itself? Preparing its own obsolescence? Public opinion's distrust of corporations has reached unheard of levels. The recent discovery that the food supply chains are out of control merely reinforces this impression.

Contemporary marketing shows us how difficult it is to call into question rules that have been rendered obsolete by incessant economic and social development. Paradoxically, marketing, due to its propensity to repeat itself, has stupidly painted itself into a corner. Although it claims to forecast the future, it is like a clairvoyant who has lost their powers but stubbornly insists on giving advice to their customers, who become more sceptical each passing day. Marketing, a big, crazy way of thinking and doing is both the offspring and parent of an economic system that is flying full speed ahead with nobody at the controls.

It is time to take action and stop this insanity.

Let us not forget that marketing and advertising are neither independent entities nor pervasive occult powers. They are merely part of the modus operandi of organizations wanting to influence individual's behaviour in ways that align with their objectives. And if this modus operandi is wrong, it is these organizations that must question themselves – clean up their acts, rethink their missions and how they relate to their audiences. Society's contempt for marketing is only a symptom. Organizations are apprehensive about their future. They would do well to listen more attentively to their audiences, whose life perspectives have shifted.

This is because the public are now taking the lead. When a system fails expectations, then its stakeholders become motivated to respond. Some will respond with withdrawal or defeatism but others will respond by taking action and generating new hope. Each day, we see more consumers making decisions, making demands, speaking out, condemning, boycotting, and organizing. Consumers are emancipating themselves with energy and enthusiasm. They are announcing new demands. Their lives are admittedly constrained by crisis, but they carry on nonetheless. They develop and think in implicatives, they seek meaning, and commitment to a better way, increasingly play as a team, and are inventing a new society.

Understanding this public and supporting its desires – this is the magnificent challenge that faces marketers and the organizations they serve today. It is high time we got rid of habits ingrained during the postwar growth between 1945 and 1975 and became more deeply committed to an urgently required transition.

It is time for both marketers and consumers to abandon deeply entrenched habits, stop being starry eyed and, instead, recognize that life brings new solutions. If we look at the cards we have been dealt, we can imagine an entirely new approach to the market: a lucid, open, constructive, responsible, and respectful approach capable of reestablishing the confidence undermined by past and current practices.

Moving toward a sustainable model of marketing requires a change in consumer behaviour. Although the individual has already made progress in this direction, many behavioural patterns remain firmly entrenched. Two or three generations and a powerful market system have shaped our nature and our behaviour. Reversals, however, are possible – even fast ones.

Corporations wishing to adopt a new approach will have to support consumers and find the right means of attaining such social development. They must ensure that marketing is no longer conducted for the sole benefit of the company.

This is not about trying to replace one sort of manipulation with another but, instead, about proposing cooperation between corporations and consumers. It is about being in a relationship, about placing the message in the public sphere by ensuring the involvement of all parties. It is, contrary to what advertising has been proposing for far too long, about publicity. Because explanations no longer suffice. Sharing and coproduction are the keys to the new logic. The purpose of cooperation is for progress to be shared among individuals who demand respect and among corporations that must become worthy of respect.

So, let us forget about twentieth-century marketing. Instead, let us think about new paths, creating meaning and relationships of which one can be proud. Like a type of post-marketing, perhaps? One that has transverse logics, one that takes everything into account, one based on a responsible market worthy of respect.

Imagine a positive and constructive sort of marketing that can satisfy new human yearnings, a sort of marketing that is sustainable and valuable for corporations. This requires rethinking traditional models and changing entrenched practices. Corporations should take advantage of these new opportunities to reconnect with their audiences and perhaps even with themselves, to regenerate overall consistency, commit, and train their respective supply chains in improved processes.

What we propose is to use marketing to involve others and to become involved ourselves. It must be done and it is tough to do. Tough to do but oh so thrilling! And on the double, too! Because the World has changed. And it will go on changing. A lot.

## Notes

1 See www.greenpeace.org/france/fr/getinvolved/Zara and www.greenpeace.org/france/fr/campagnes/ Toxique/Toxic-Threads/Levis.
2 On April 24, 2013, in Dhaka, Bangladesh, a building housing several garment factories, whose output was destined for major international brands, collapsed causing over 1,135 deaths.

# 1 Marketing's headlong rush

*The consumer is questioned and the consumer answers.*
*But it seems that nobody really understands what the consumer is saying.*
*They listen but hear nothing.*

Oh, how comfortable it was, a few years ago, to start a marketing course with a debate on the concept of need. It was therefore easy to seek shelter behind the classical theory of consumer sovereignty, which can be summarized as follows: consumers are well informed and eager to improve their welfare and they tell manufacturers what merchandise to produce.

In accordance with this view, marketing and advertising serve the sole purpose of drawing potential buyers' attention to a given product and making them prefer one brand over another. The outcome has been a somewhat cursory debate that has tended to make consumers responsible for their own choices without really questioning the system as a whole: "One person's needs are not necessarily the same as another's". "Who can judge whether a need is true or false?" "Has anyone forced you to buy a cell phone or an Internet connection?" By implying that marketing merely satisfies our desires, it has been simple, indeed simplistic, to posit the consumer's responsibility as an essential factor of our consumption!

Conversely, it would be quite easy nowadays to assume an exclusively critical attitude and blame marketing for all problems, to relieve the consumer of any responsibility. That would be just as easy and would perfectly match the current trend in public opinion of demonizing marketing. Come September, the first word more than half of my new students associate with marketing is *deceit*.

Let us try, instead, to understand how, in less than a century, marketing – and, more generally, the Western industrial and commercial complex – has been able to promise happiness by virtue of possessions, a promise that is constantly renewed, with increasing swiftness, recklessly squandering the World's resources, an issue that was barely mentioned before.

If marketing has become a dirty word, synonymous with trickery, easy profits, and destructive short-termism, then its nature becomes an object worthy of curiosity. It is well worth our while to inspect its mechanisms, the successive stages of their development, and the blunders they cause and from these extract designs for paths to true progress.

Let us begin by putting marketing in its proper place: its function is "merely" to enforce the workings of the economic system. It has no independent existence by itself. It is not an evil supervillain. It often falls flat on its face. From the standpoint of economic history, marketing is a recent phenomenon. Most importantly, it is no more than what people make of it.

## From Boucicaut to instant mashed potatoes

To understand the mechanisms of modern consumption, we must remind ourselves that, until quite recently, humans could not afford to consume any products other than those enabling them merely to survive, at least as far as most of the population was concerned. In France, it was the Industrial Revolution, associated with a rearrangement of commerce, that enabled people to purchase the labour of others for their own comfort and pleasure. When Aristide Boucicaut founded Le Bon Marché department store in Paris in 1852,[1] he was most likely unaware that he would, among other things, alter the market's power relations between commerce and manufacturing, change the role and image of women in society, and pave the way for mass consumption.

By offering a permanent renewal of seductive products destined for a new bourgeois class, department stores invented the concept of what we, today, call shopping. They invented the ephemeral pleasure of owning something new and shiny and, as a corollary, the permanent unease given the need to consistently adapt to new models. No marketing existed yet, in either concept or name. However, there is no doubt that the urge to trade, born of envy and frustration, lurked beneath the surface and, for the first time, large-scale manufacturing created a standard that could be propagated by the ever-expanding printing press. The manufacture of standardized desire had begun.

During that period, advertising stumbled clumsily along and the public's judgment was uneven. However, around 1900, a new generation of advertisers arose who deployed all their energy into experimenting with techniques that engendered the first brands. Thus, the art of selling entered a new era: the age of differentiation.

Its primary purpose was to create preferences and, in the process, the foundations of marketing were laid. Thereafter, the issue was no longer whether you owned a car but, instead, whether you owned a Citroën or a Renault, whether you wash yourself with Ivory soap or have discovered Nivea cream's blue can. So, when Michelin[2] and its brand-new Michelin Man (also known as Bibendum) started selling tyres, encouraging the owners of the first automobiles to travel in them was an urgent task, for example, by making them tour the countryside. The Michelin Guide was designed with this purpose in mind.

At the turn of the twentieth century came home appliances, a proliferation of toiletries, tourism, ready-to-wear clothing, leisure activities, and so forth. A swarm of new temptations, improved comfort, and living conditions that became increasingly available to less prosperous members of society were led by a new style of marketing that arose in the United States toward the middle of the twentieth century.

The 1950s brought forth a new society, driven by technological progress and scarred by war, that placed its hopes in the future. Everyday life was transformed by electricity, the automobile offered freedom, and we would soon travel to the moon. Increasing standards of living and urbanization constantly created new opportunities that consumed huge amounts of petroleum, chemical fertilizers, and plastics.

Maslow's hierarchy,[3] first published in 1943, depicts the logic of human desires and motivations in a model that can be readily transposed to buying behaviour. Once physiological and security needs have been satisfied, group identity becomes the central issue. This swiftly brought forth the single-family home, the fully equipped kitchen, the family sedan, and camping holidays.[4]

In the 1960s, when international trade spread, supply grew tenfold, forcing marketing specialists to develop new techniques. Market studies then enabled an improved understanding of consumers who no longer lacked life's basic amenities. Accordingly, marketing was probed, explored, and analysed to create demand that seemed infinitely adjustable. Marketing relied on the development of television and tempting offers of consumer credit.

The leading role in the new consumer drama was played by the homemaker. The homemaker was so heavily burdened with nurturing responsibilities and so subject to social pressure to conform that he or she was an ideal target. The detergent and food industries, among others, began to offer with great enthusiasm new products ostensibly intended to simplify the homemaker's life. There was trust and everything was modern. Long live supermarkets, enzyme detergent, and mashed potato flakes![5] While most homemakers were assumed to be women, men were by no means neglected. Tobacco products, alcoholic beverages, and cars announced his standing as a modern man.

The race for the accumulation of possessions had begun. The 1970s would entrench this phenomenon and, in the 1980s, the supermarket became a superstore. The neighbourhood hardware store was renamed a specialized superstore. The mall seized power. The Austin Mini and the Renault 4L were replaced by a Japanese 4 × 4. Advertising began playing the leading role on specialized shows shown on TV sets with pointy corners.

These years of ostentation, conspicuous consumption, and glittery advertising were the glory years of media moguls, Rupert Murdoch and Robert Maxwell, or the symbolic figure Gordon Gekko (and other nicely tanned advertising executives and business people).

Then, the beginning of the 1990s began looking gloomy:
For 50 years, save for 1993, people have consumed a little more each year, so that today the annual volume of consumption per person is three times that of 1960. However, starting in the mid-1970s, France made a transition from the Thirty Glorious Years, characterized by the development of mass consumption, to a period of far slower growth in terms of purchasing power and consumption.[6]

## Economic crisis or crisis of faith?

Granted, the economic crisis of 1991 was not the first, but it profoundly changed the situation. The ballyhoo surrounding the Gulf War, combined with a sense of imminent economic peril, found an outlet in consumption, not to indulge in even greater consumption but, instead – and this was the first time this occurred on such a large scale – to indict it. The standard of living had never been so high, closets had never been so crammed full. And morale had never been so low. The happiness that consumption was supposed to bring failed to materialize.

Could advertising have been lying to us? Advertising made us buy stacks of products that now seem vapid or useless. Washing machines have 40 programmes, of which we use only four. Some 70 per cent of French people own electric yogurt makers, but three-quarters of these devices have never been used. The consumers feel aggrieved and abused and are beginning to reconsider their propensity to consume, but the very same advertising promptly brings them back into line. Advertising does not hesitate to invoke the consumer's responsibility for solving the crisis: the consumer must consume, of course, to turn the wheels of the economy. The consumer is thus made to feel guilty. At the very moment the consumer is prepared to question the system's validity, he or she is told to slip another quarter into the slot because otherwise the situation will become worse. And, in this context, this is perfectly true:[7]

Some agencies, especially in the United States, go for broke: it is no longer even a matter of praising a given product, you have to buy anything, but above all buy, to strengthen consumer confidence in the US economy: "Buy something!" says this ad for automaker Range Rover. *"Of course, we would prefer that you buy a Range Rover"*, the advertising copy continues.

But if there is no chance of this happening, then buy a microwave oven. A basset hound. Theater tickets. Candy. Anything, because if we wait until the recession is officially over to make us spend again, the crisis will never be solved.

Jean-Louis Peytavin, 1991

Although the 1990s marked a shift in consumer thinking and behaviour, the underlying business model had not been called into question. The marketing juggernaut believed that merely changing the message and offering more products in fancy wrappers would suffice to put the consumer back on the path of hyperconsumption.

It would take brands another two decades to understand consumers, who were filled with new desires and beginning to consider their environment (in the broad sense of the term) and the consequences of their consumer choices. Omens of impending environmental misfortune succeeded each other at a pace that grew swifter with each passing decade. In 1990, for the first time a minister of the environment who belonged to the environmentalist movement was appointed in France. For the first time, the act of purchasing was associated with its socioeconomic consequences: if I buy a product at the superstore for less, it is because the brand buys it for less from the manufacturer, who could be my neighbour, or it buys it from the other side of the World, potentially putting my job at stake. The crisis, my consumption, my purchasing power – everything is linked. On the other hand, everything is set up to lead me into temptation.

However, the marketing establishment is not going to pay any attention to this incipient consumer awareness threatening the system's continuity. On the contrary: it will do everything in its power to distract us from the problem or exploit it for its own benefit. Its ability to listen is showing the initial signs of fatigue. New sham products and bogus advertising are deployed to dispel fear and delay making the necessary changes, in the knowledge that these changes will be even more painful tomorrow than today.

The entire assortment of pristine products invading our supermarket shelves was a token of this purely opportunistic adjustment of marketing messages. These supposedly pure products – shampoos, detergents, soft drinks – were condemned to failure. The marketing of "natural products" (i.e., without preservatives, dyes, or parabens) had not yet been born, but the marketing of "apparently without products" was in full swing!

Advertising copy followed suit. Then came the first advertising campaigns to claim that the merchandise touted was natural and protected the environment. Advertising had learned how to greenwash. The content of auto advertising was also challenged. The goal was to emphasize selling products more relevant to consumers' lives and their new concerns.

The advertising of French car manufacturers adopted a refreshing new tone. Citroën ceased vaunting horsepower and began praising clever consumers. It changed its 1980s advertising slogans and began talking about the Great Wall of China and aircraft carriers.[8] Eventually, in 1993, Citroën announced that its AX model car was nothing less than "The car owned by people who don't put all their money into their cars".[9] Renault, not to be outdone, challenged the consumer by launching the Twingo: "It's up to you to invent the life that goes with it".[10]

As if to lubricate the workings of the consumption machine, the message has intermittently changed. Officials have periodically soothed popular anxiety with reassuring announcements to the effect that the necessary measures have already been put into effect. Such stopgaps could have sufficed to dispel momentary gloom, bolster consumer confidence, or allay panic – but in vain, alas!

Because it was not just momentary gloom; it was, instead, the beginning of true awareness. It was the birth of the alter-consumer, who has since multiplied throughout Europe and North America and who easily eludes standard marketing ploys. Eric Fouquier, founder of the Théma think tank, has spent 20 years analysing alter-consumer shopping behaviour:

> Critical, subtle, idealistic. They invest their purchasing power outside the well-trodden paths of traditional marketing, instead adhering to a certain ethic and respect for the environment. They are sceptical of brands and of advertising. Including the sustainable development pitch incessantly repeated by corporations. They trust the social media buzz more than they do the merchandise wrappers proclaiming 100% ecological purity.... They are the alter-consumers, the adversaries of hyper-consumers prone to impulse buying and always in search of novelty.
>
> They began to make themselves heard in the early 1960s, but their numbers have grown steadily, driven by crises of the food supply and of the environment, since the movement, initially launched by a coterie of intellectuals, has become diversified and now thrives in all social classes and occupational groups. Moreover, it is an international movement.... There are alter-consumers in the United States, Japan

and Australia, as well as in other European countries. Consequently an 'alter-marketing' must be invented to target these consumers. This is a major challenge for retailers, whose credibility has dwindled so dramatically of late. As a matter of fact, they have become quite vulnerable.[11]

We can confidently assume that the first people to display such responsible consumer behaviour did so driven by a quest for personal fulfilment. Taking such a step requires no great effort on the part of those who are free to choose, thanks to their privileged social, financial, or cultural status. Some commentators have condescendingly labelled this new sort of market participant the *bobo* (i.e., bourgeois–bohemian) consumer, considering such consumers' behaviour merely a pose that allows them to signal their virtue, claim social prestige, and shrug off guilt.

However, the facts prove that this consumption pattern is not restricted to a narrow, urban, and privileged social group, as commonly assumed. Today, responsible consumption patterns characterize an extremely varied range of consumer profiles, including the most disadvantaged.

Commenting on the report "Low-income French people with sustainable consumption patterns" of October 2012, the Observatory of the BoP (Base of the Pyramid)[12] states,

> Driven by the wish to "improve their habits of consumption," especially in terms of health, many people who lead precarious lives are ready, indeed eager for change. Many adopt sustainable consumption patterns in response to pressure from their family, especially from their children. Nearly one-fourth of them believe that supermarkets have an important role to play in terms of raising awareness, but the majority finds fault with the information conveyed there, finding it far too intricate and complex.

Changes in consumption habits are not (or no longer perhaps) motivated by consumers' desire to soothe their conscience. Instead, they are challenges to a model that has not lived up to expectations. And, contrary to what one might think, the economic crisis has merely strengthened these changes, due to factors that have only recently become relevant. This is because adopting these new habits enables the discovery of solutions, such as the consumption of locally sourced products or second-hand purchases, which allow for a balance between personal benefits and collective interests.

Changes in consumers' consumption patterns are intended to ensure their safety and health, earn them the respect of their fellow citizens, and, ideally, strengthen their social linkages. Marketing, fossilized within its outdated model, flounders in a saturated market. Moreover, the marketing establishment often fights the wrong foe.

## Marketing is going around in circles

### The undifferentiation crisis

With saturated markets and saturated consumers, what options offer hope of renewed economic growth? New products daily? But innovation does not consist in merely waving a magic wand.

And the marketing of new products has also harmed those who undertook it. All corporations have the same goal: differentiation. Strangely enough, their differentiation plans are all based on the same studies and the same methods and are hampered by the same fear of being wrong, because every mistake is costly. Therefore, shockingly, what must happen inevitably happens: the market is standardized and supply becomes uniform.

When the conventions of a market sector have been adjusted, managers tend to preserve them indefinitely for fear of incurring risks through innovation. Go to an electrical appliance store and examine the assortment of irons offered. They all have the same design. They are all white and blue. More professional models are grey and made of stainless steel. What do consumers expect? Maybe that is what they are used to. Now examine the assortment of vacuum cleaners: heavy-duty vacuum cleaners are red and quiet vacuum cleaners are blue. However, those who strayed from the herd have been richly rewarded for their daring. Dyson chose breakthrough technology and painted its vacuum cleaner yellow, thus creating the high-end vacuum cleaner market. Additionally, the PC market took off when Apple realized that computers need not be ugly beige contraptions. The brand even turned its products into objects of sensual desire!

Fearful executives, saturated colour codes, antiquated standards of consumption. Marketing is going around in circles and seems to ignore the consumer's new desires.

### Absurd supply and misunderstood insights

Marketing's goal is usually to awaken in the consumer an unquenchable desire for a product. We see how little success is being achieved on this score when we examine the new products offered at the Paris International Agribusiness Show: brownie chips, madeleine-flavoured syrup, yogurt for men, and liquid salt. Curiously, these fanciful products are called marketing; however, the opposite is true, since they are not driven by any real motivation. Efforts to innovate often stumble over the reality of consumers who, while seeking novelty and pleasure, are nonetheless fortunately endowed with a modicum of common sense.

One might think that these attempts are made by small firms, ill-equipped to conduct market research, that believe in a brilliant concept or in the existence of a market gap. While that occasionally happens, the big names in manufacturing fail just as often. When the market is out of breath, marketing teams devote colossal amounts of energy to dissecting consumers to the point where even a casual remark by a consumer can trigger extremely costly product development efforts. The search for "consumer insight", which can be defined as an expectation linked to experience, has therefore become the last hope of marketing departments.[13]

One can imagine how much energy is devoted to monitoring and analysing consumers' most trivial actions, gestures, and thoughts to finally hit on THE BIG IDEA. Thus, products and sales pitches arise that ultimately focus on a single detail, a harebrained or plausible expectation that is actually irrelevant to consumer habits, and they wind up with an artificial concept that the consumer leaves on the shelf. The following are two examples from the field of dairy products, namely, Mammoth yogurt for men and Essensis anti-aging yogurt.

## Mammoth: super-square

When men and women were asked which milk product they consumed the most, 40 per cent of women and 35 per cent of men answered yogurt, with yogurt being perceived as rather feminine and men saying they preferred milk, which ranked second. So be it. It is well known that opinion surveys cannot tell whether a respondent is lying or not. Consequently, manufacturers would be well advised to make their products more masculine so that men will buy them. This is what a New Zealand brand attempted when it launched Mammoth yogurt, which, in the company's own words, was "designed to" dispel male reluctance to eat yogurt. It had a thick texture, containing seeds and cereals, all in a large square pot with a spoon built into the lid. Rolled out in France in November 2012, Mammoth apparently never even reached the dairy shelves. But not to worry! An American brand has launched Powerful Yogurt, the yogurt for men that helps grow your abs: "Powerful is the voice of your abs flexing".

## Essensis: youth in a jar ... of yogurt

No need here for any sophisticated market research: eternal youth is a core expectation of consumers. Inspired by this endeavour and by successful Asian experimentation with cosmetic food, Danone launched Essensis in February 2007, a yogurt that "nourishes the skin from the inside",[14] a promise that can only be well received in consumer focus groups. On paper, at least. Because the reality was entirely different: presented as an up-and-coming best seller comparable to Actimel, Essensis yogurt flouted food marketing conventions with its pink bottle worthy of a perfume. Essensis was rolled out with a mass media advertising campaign to the tune of €10 million. Weary and disappointed by poor sales, Danone eventually announced its withdrawal from the market in February 2009.

Nonetheless, back in 2007, consumers had expressed expectations of simplicity, naturalness, a return to traditional food – not a magic product, which, of course, Essensis was not.

The consumer is questioned and the consumer answers. But it seems that nobody really understands what the consumer is saying. They listen but hear nothing.

## Irresponsible supply

Obviously, consumers expect something different and they especially do not expect to be treated as if they were consumers and nothing more. Moreover, the products supplied are often deplorable. Marketing does one of two things: either it mentions only prices or it announces bogus innovations, with vapid and useless bells and whistles. Both of these marketing approaches raise serious doubts about the opinions manufacturing executives hold of their fellow citizens. Are they just nincompoops ready to accept whatever comes their way because it is cheap, or are they eager to buy some flimsy item with no redeeming value simply because it is new?

There can be no doubt that we are well and truly in the midst of an economic crisis. Admittedly, the consumer's budget is tighter than ever. (For some, living conditions are not even decent anymore; however, these people are not the intended targets of marketing messages.) Under the pretext of savings, our society's most prized values are incidentally being undermined.

Take a recent insurance offer, for example: "Just pay for your own risk, and not a penny more". It looks attractive at first glance. After all, insurance is a big-ticket item these days. But let us take a step back and analyse the concept of insurance itself. Insurance involves a group of people together making small contributions against foreseeable risks to protect whomever winds up needing help. Well, then, what is insurance that covers only one's own risk? For the insured, does it mean every man for himself instead of collective security, just to save a few dozen euros? Is this saving really worth the risk of discovering on the day something happens that you don't qualify for the protection?

The insurance company is riding the low-cost fad, playing on the hyper-individualization of motivations, which is so easy to trigger in times of crisis. Is this still insurance? This no longer has anything to do with the idea of pooling risks.

However, price is not the sole incentive tempting potential customers; convenience is also a big draw. "More convenient!" "Faster!" The arguments are not lacking to make us pay prices that are sometimes exorbitant but difficult to compare with those of rival products. For example, you can now make chocolate cake with a premixed powder that comes in a box. What's in the box? One bag of raw chocolate flakes and one bag labelled *cake mix*.

Now all you have to do is get some butter and eggs, which are not included in the package, and add them to the mix. So, you already need to have butter and eggs on hand. That is not very convenient for someone who never cooks. But what is in the mix? Flour, sugar, and baking powder? Wow, that really is a new product! We probably did not know that these ingredients were needed to make a chocolate cake, but they cost a lot more money this way: three times more for the chocolate and ten times more for the flour. So, we have bogus homemade cake that is not terribly convenient, is much more expensive, and requires twice as much packaging. A magnificent success, don't you think?

This example might make you smile. It does not seem like such a big deal; yet it questions the consumer's common sense. More importantly, it casts doubt on the ethics and sincerity of the manufacturer, whose website, called "Cultivating pleasure in better ways", explains that its chocolate comes from the company's own supply chain and that 30,000 farmers were trained (no mention of what they were trained in) thanks to its Chocolate Project. Moreover, we learn that working and living conditions have improved (who knows how), that work is being done on the packaging (indeed!), and that shippers have become more respectful. While announcing such ethical breakthroughs, why not explain to consumers that they can make a chocolate cake all by themselves, with a certain chocolate bar of the same brand, by sharing simple recipes, without the need for a purchase, without particular packaging, without all the useless fuss that treats them like idiots and makes them pay dearly for the privilege? Does the brand really believe that this is the way to build lasting trust? In Chapter 4, we will again discuss the issue of how consistent the brand's contract is.

### Genuine co-production versus fake co-production

Among new marketing methods, co-production is beginning to take hold or, rather, is starting to develop. "Customize your Nikes!" "Help choose Danette's next fragrance!" "Become a co-producer!"

People are co-producers every time they contribute to the production of products or services, so it is not really such a brand-new idea:

- Since the 1940s, self-service retailers have been putting the consumer to work.
- Since the 1980s, we have been withdrawing cash from ATMs and filling our gas tanks by ourselves.
- Fast food establishments provided the template for co-produced catering by having us serve our own tables.
- IKEA has made a fortune by letting us assemble our own furniture.
- Airlines allow us to handle our own ticket purchases and bookings.
- Internet helplines hold our hands while we fix flat tires on our own.

We have gradually and quite easily adjusted to these practices for the sake of saving money, self-reliance, saving time, convenience, or personal satisfaction. Additionally, advertisers have managed to translate them into attractive promises:

"Thanks to online banking, your bank never closes".
"Choose a sandwich, a drink, and a toy for your enjoyment".
"Increase your chances of winning by providing the names and addresses of five people".
"Audition for the next TV commercial".
"Create the new Doritos commercial".

The principle is now exploited by the advertising industry and by platforms devoted to co-creation, which can be a source of enjoyment and satisfaction, as well as new acquaintances. However, it usually implies that the producer provides fewer services and saves on costs: fewer employees at the counter, fewer points of sale, less time spent with customers, no staff needed in the restaurant, and no more gas station attendants.

As labour sociologist Marie-Anne Dujarier explains, the consumer has gradually become a segment of the labour pool that is not only available free of charge but also eager and motivated![15] Accordingly, co-production involves adjustments on the part of the producer, as well as the management of this new human resource, including splitting the work into simple tasks (ready-to-assemble furniture that comes with instructions and a small custom tool), convenient human–machine interfaces (cashier-less super-market checkouts), and suitable management tools to handle consumers (assessment, encouragement, competition).

And consumers find themselves inputting their friends' information to augment the brand's database of prospective customers!

Nowadays it is hard to imagine living without ATMs or without pur-chasing airline tickets online, because doing such things yourself is gener-ally considered an act of self-reliance and a time saving. However, the underlying principle seems dubious at best. Is the consumer actually empowered in any way by expending labour in this fashion? As a matter of fact, unpaid co-production seems somehow immoral. So, how should "incompetent" consumers (the digitally illiterate, those with a poor command of the language, the visually impaired) be treated?

Finally, in creative co-production (e.g., co-creating a logo, an advert-ising campaign, a recipe), what are the real places of design and innova-tion in the company? Are we involved in a simple advertising operation? Does the company actually put the consumer in the position of creator? How should the value produced be managed and the proceeds equitably distributed?

In their quest for self-reliance, do consumers truly appreciate their own power and the value of their work? Nonetheless, co-production can be a path to a new sort of marketing, as long as you do not consider it a mere advertising pitch or just a way to cut costs. Co-production based on an obsolete model only impoverishes people further.

Based on this short survey of the period from 1900 until today, we can readily identify marketing's various stages during its brief existence and the mistakes it has made. Exuberance, crises, the constant recycling of out-dated models, short-termism – today, marketing is reaching the end of its tether. Within a changing overall context, traditional models seem strangely outdated and no longer generate the desired outcomes. Instead, they lead to their own downfall. Marketing causes rejection. Unsuitable applications, denial of a changed society, the World's complexity, and its new challenges have exceeded marketing's ability to cope.

## Notes

1 See Michael B. Miller (trans. Jacques Chabert) (1987), *Au Bon Marché (1869–1920): le Consommateur Apprivoisé* [The Bon Marché: Bourgeois Culture and the Department Store, 1869–1920], Paris, Armand Colin.
2 Michelin's slogan was "The tyre that drinks up obstacles" ("*le pneu qui boit l'obstacle*").
3 A.H. Maslow, "A Theory of Human Motivation", *Psychological Review*, 50, 1943, pp. 370–396; see also http.maslow.com.

4  Much criticized since then, Maslow's proposal gave a simple, almost universal explanation for what "should" motivate people. It is still taught and remains a reference for many managers.

5  *L'essor de la grande distribution*, as www.ina.fr/video/I12248851.

6  National Institute of Statistics and Economic Studies (*Institut national de la statistique et des études économiques*), *La consommation des ménages depuis cinquante ans*, Georges Consales, Maryse Fesseau, and Vladimir Passeron.

7  Jean-Louis Peytavin, *"Années 90: la crise de la publicité. Fin de la poudre aux yeux, retour à l'authentique"*. Quaderni 16, winter 1991–92. *"La vulgarisation des sciences humaines"*.

8  See  www.youtube.com/watch?v=WXbHb3YhBLA  and  www.youtube.com/watch?v=4QOB1uBboSQ.

9  See www.youtube.com/watch?v=i4N-kHnrvRg.

10 See www.youtube.com/watch?v=dXJFEPDYM9A.

11 Anne Bariet, L'Entreprise.com, March 27, 2013, at https://lentreprise.lexpress.fr/rh-management/marketing-comment-cibler-l-alter-consommateur_1523036.html.

12 The base consists of enterprise, poverty, and development. See http://bopobs.com.

13 See http://archives.lesechos.fr/archives/cercle/2011/11/30/cercle_40636.htm.

14 See www.youtube.com/watch?v=RPo47jpeftc.

15 M.-A. Dujarier, *"Le travail du consommateur"*, La Découverte, 2008.

# 2 Complexity killed the marketing mix

*What is the use of constant product availability if the supply – and hence meaning – does not keep up with it?*

## The end of the four Ps

The dominant marketing model is a bag of tricks called the marketing mix, namely product, price, place, and promotion. Although this model has yielded good results for over 50 years, today it is no longer capable of satisfying exacting consumers and corporations struggling with economic and ecological challenges. This model is incapable of resolving the issues that are now at stake and satisfying more discriminating values, since each of its four attributes has become more complex and has altered its logic, organization, support, and context to the point where continuing to add these four Ps no longer enables change. This logic, as we have seen in new products, sometimes even renders the supply of products absurd and unsuited to our new World. The picture is fuzzy: price is no longer a benchmark, the store is no longer the only place for purchases, and newly manufactured products compete with second-hand ones or the 3D printer. Different analyses and visions are needed.

## Prices: where are the benchmarks?

It has become customary in recent years to believe that consumers are only interested in getting the lowest possible price. The consumer has indeed become an expert at finding bargains. But this single view of the facts is reductive, especially because its software of choice is actually much more complex. The rules of pricing and the symbolic and traditional values of prices have been obliterated. The very concept of price has become utterly fuzzy and indistinct.

## Do prices always rise?

Depending on the business cycle, price is the focus of consumer discussion. Comparisons have become a daily pastime. This creates a paradox, since many products have never been cheaper while the general impression is that of an overall rise in prices. How can we explain this?[1]

First, in Europe, the switch to the euro was an important psychological threshold and the prices of everyday products increased. A cup of coffee at the corner bar rose from FF10 to €2 (FF15) in one year. However, last winter we also found a very trendy woollen bonnet for €0.99 and a flight from Paris to Marseille for €19.

Why do we feel that the cost of living has increased? Because the feeling of economic pressure grows in proportion to the true or apparent lack of money available to buy everyday products. This is because the money is spent elsewhere: ten years ago, a telephone line from the national telephone company cost a household a few dozen euros, whereas nowadays owning a mobile phone costs close to €600 a year.[2] Additionally, each family has about seven mobile phones, on average. Consumer spending on electronic gadgets plus their accessories, upkeep, and connection has been growing at a dizzying pace and we have become addicted to them. Assuming, realistically, that incomes remain stagnant, this surging outlay on gadgets makes us skimp on more pedestrian expenses such as groceries.

## The disconnect between prices and value and the search for products

In a context of new trade-offs and a decoupling of value from price, new merchandise has become available, making it even more difficult for consumers to budget their expenses.

## The delusion of free stuff

Let us start with online services. It is hard to explain to a teenager that Google and Facebook are corporations seeking to maximize their profits and that the music must be paid for, since it is only a click away. New business models have disrupted our perception of value. Thus, although we are willing to pay a high price for communication devices such as smartphones, tablets, and other terminals, we are reluctant to take the step of purchasing content. For example, dematerialization has made it more difficult to sell music. Therefore, to find a sustainable business model, corporations have invented freemium, which means making some of the content available for free but reserving the most tempting items for paying subscribers. We are still learning how these new models work. After being told that they can access content for free, consumers are then informed they must pay after all. Since the transition from free content to premium content has dematerialized, easily, with no card or paper required, and the amounts involved are often paltry, freemium seems less real – and therefore less painful.

In real life, stuff is also sometimes offered for free, or nearly free. In the eyeglasses market, it has become standard practice to give paying customers a second and sometimes even a third set of eyeglasses for free. GPS devices are often available in cars for a symbolic euro. What are these products worth? How can we avoid considering them disposable items? How relevant is marketing when it must offer more and more products just to sell a single one?

### *Supposedly painless payment methods and the dilution effect*

A driver's licence or a computer for one euro a day are merely loans that must be paid back in monthly instalments. Banks rely on such gimmicks to persuade young people to open accounts.

### *Unlimited offers*

For many years, public transit has offered unlimited travel to season ticket holders. Unlimited usage is now also offered to users of mobile phones and movie spectators. And our loyalty is assured.

### *A new kind of subscription: mixed-product assortments*

How can a business make sure it will receive a share of a consumer's budget? Through subscriptions of course, by giving consumers the impression of receiving a monthly gift! Reviving the book club model, which once seemed obsolete, for €10 a month you can now receive a charming box of miniature cosmetic products. These are graciously supplied by cosmetics brands so they can advertise their novelties. The participants are expected to gush about the new items in online beauty forums and unboxing videos (videos in which Youtubers stage themselves when they receive their deliveries and comment on their opening and discovery of contents).

The Orchestra children's clothing line resorts to a slightly different expedient, granting a 50 per cent discount all year round to customers who become subscribers. Why buy elsewhere? It would be interesting to observe how this subscriber-brand relationship develops. The bond linking

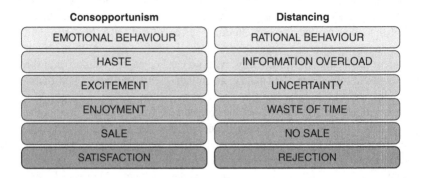

*Figure 2.1* Price and consumer.

them ensnares the consumer and changes his or her buying attitudes. When consumer choice is restricted, what happens to participation? Are pleasure and satisfaction the same thing? How significant is the restriction? And at what savings?

### Opportunism or aloofness?

When price is no longer the principal criterion, "traditional products" suddenly seem expensive. Buying cheaper becomes a national sport and a source of satisfaction even greater than possessing the coveted object. This distancing of the product generates new ways of thinking and behaviour. Finding a good deal is just as satisfying as actually consummating the transaction.

For some consumers, so-called "consopportunists", emotion overwhelms reason when their quest – from brick and mortar stores to online merchants, from auction sites to one-off trades between individuals – becomes more meaningful and more satisfying than the outcome. A change then takes place in the timeline of the purchase. Whereas the search for the coveted item can drag on for weeks, once it is found, by contrast, the ensuing transaction can be consummated in breathless haste. It is the transaction itself that is fulfilling.

However, de-emphasizing the merchandise is also likely to reduce its consumption when opportunities for comparison seem endless and sources of supply ubiquitous: in regular stores, online, on international websites, from traditional retail chains, and from discounters and destockers. The task seems immense and endless and invariably discouraging. When price wars, comparisons, and the impression of getting a good deal turn into a labyrinth, some consumers prefer to place their values elsewhere than in consumption, repelled by the waste of time and energy involved and ultimately disappointed by their purchases.

### New proposals for average pricing: security, satisfaction, and social guarantee

In the 1990s, the volume of consumers for each range level was reversed (see Figure 2.2). The middle range was, for many years, the core of the market. The main consumer brands had successfully ensconced themselves in the mid-range niche. The high end was reserved for exceptional purchases or for a tiny elite. The low end satisfied only a handful of very low-income consumers.

It is worthwhile analysing this inversion of the model, although it could seem to be a caricature. When exposed to financial constraint, the consumer must make trade-offs. If consumers are forced to satisfy most of their consumption needs with cheap products, they will make up for the sacrifice by periodically consuming a more expensive product. They will buy groceries both at hard discount outlets and at exclusive delicatessens, perhaps even on the same day. On the one hand, the principal motivation is low prices; on the other, consumers seek a particular quality of product with real added value or else they covet a brand that confers social distinction. This trend entails the fragmentation of the consumer, who thus ceases to be a monolith. The consumer has become legion and is exercising the power of choice.

But then what has become of the middle range? The mid-range has lost its mojo. Its greater usefulness does not compensate for its higher price.

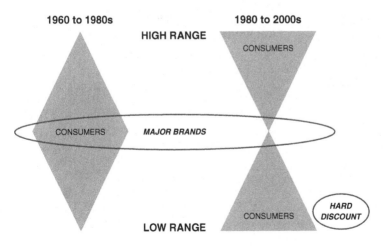

*Figure 2.2* Consumer and range levels, 1960–2010.

All cars, even cheap ones, feature power windows, power steering, and air conditioning. All foodstuffs, even the cheapest on the bottom shelves, must comply with food and health codes.

Note that, if mid-range products have lost their attraction for the time being, it is because their previously advantageous traits have been diluted and marketers have failed to keep them in a dominant position. A new era is beginning in which the mid-range is recovering its aura, thanks to the efforts of new players and the development of new products (see Figure 2.3).

The concept of mid-range products also encompasses products that fulfil new expectations better than traditional products, products of proven quality with a long useful life, without frills but offering new features. The consumer is familiar with the product and knows where it was made. It is healthy and safe and prevents waste. It is not the cheapest product, but it might be the most satisfactory one.

## And where can this item be bought now?

A headline in *Le Monde* noted, "The French still shop at superstores (but reluctantly)".[3] Another staple of the marketing mix, place, also shows it has undergone major changes, starting with a crisis of the large retailer business model. Superstores spearheaded mass consumption but their turnover has been declining since 2009 and they now seem to be petering out. Supermarkets, smaller than superstores, are better able to withstand the downturn. Nonetheless, both superstores and supermarkets are at odds with consumers. For one in three consumers, shopping has become a trying experience.

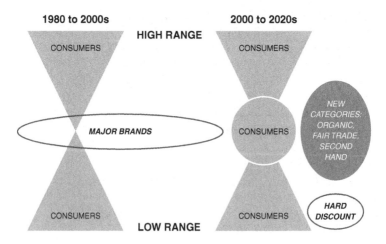

*Figure 2.3* Consumer and range levels, 1960–2020.

*Are big chain stores finished?*

According to a 1979 article in *Distribution d'aujourd'hui*,

> In 1958 Professor Malcolm P. McNair announced his wheel of retailing theory. McNair describes successive stages in the historical development of retailing. In a nutshell, McNair[4] finds that as time goes by, retail trade goes through several stages. In each stage of retail development several retail business models coexist in an unstable equilibrium that is then disrupted by a new business model that competes successfully against the existing models. According to this theory, each successful new model has always featured low prices and drastically reduced sales margins, and has adopted methods characterized by austerity and efficiency. By putting pressure on their costs, these new retail outlets are able to compete successfully with established merchants, who have often made the mistake of trying too hard to please their customers at the same time as they raised their sales margins. But the newcomers in turn fall into the trap of upgrading their service. They raise their prices. These champions of price-cutting thus become vulnerable to competition from new retailers who again offer basic products and large savings. Thus, the wheel makes a full turn.

The commercial sector arose by following this logic: lowering prices, reducing sales margins, and raising efficiency. At the beginning of the twentieth century, the *magasin populaire* succeeded the department store by selling cheaper products on the premises, with fewer amenities. Later, the American-style cash and carry of the 1930s gave birth to the French supermarket. The introduction of self-service in stores made consumers independent and allowed stores to lay off most of their staff and cut costs and prices. After that, the superstore of the 1960s, likewise a French invention, amplified the phenomenon – until zero-service retailing arrived in the shape of hard discount outlets.

Finally, to underprice the major brands, big retail chains created private labels, originally intended for low-cost product lines. But they gradually become more sophisticated in order to differentiate themselves in terms of quality or origin and especially to retain consumers.

We know today that the rule of constantly falling prices has reached its limits and that the times when shoppers would gaze in wonder at the bounty of merchandise offered are long past. Large retail chains have lost their attractiveness. Worse yet, nowadays they are actually in disrepute: "Even more seriously, almost two out of three respondents believe that hypermarkets are partly to blame for France's economic and social crisis".[5]

Disenchantment has set in, caused by several factors. First, of course, the economic crisis, which has forced everyone to scrutinize their spending habits. However, in more general terms, in view of the low prices paid for farm products, the condemnation of restrictive social policies, and the huge number of products that are discarded or destroyed, the French have begun to reassess these temples of consumption with a more jaundiced eye. The power conferred upon these corporations by their oligopolistic status grants them vast power over even their most important suppliers.

To top it all off, the trend toward the gargantuan has eliminated all traces of humanity while the length of time shoppers spend in superstores and the size of the average shopping basket have both increased. Superstores have thus gradually created the conditions for consumers to reject and mistrust them.[6]

If supermarkets are doing better, it is because they are smaller and less dehumanized and because we spend less time in them. How we view time is a key factor in this crisis. When consumption is no longer a central issue and the constraints of daily life grow burdensome, consumers no longer enjoy shopping and tend to reduce the time they devote to this activity. Shopping is a time-consuming chore: shoppers spend an average of one hour and 57 minutes in superstores and one hour and 28 minutes per shopping trip in supermarkets.[7] Shopping time has lost all meaning and has become compulsive and frequently even unpleasant. After all, nobody is amazed anymore at seeing supermarket shelves packed with product. Nowadays, nobody in their right mind wants to spend time buying detergent and pet food. We have much better things to do.

### E-commerce has become routine

After years of announcements of a merchandising revolution, e-commerce has now become routine for consumers. Stores have ceased to be consumers' favourite buying venue, except for a minority of European consumers who reject online shopping. These consumers feel the need to be on the spot, to see and feel the merchandise. They are cautious about quality and distrustful of online payments.

E-commerce sales continue to grow at a double-digit rate, since consumers shop online with ever-greater frequency. Turnover will exceed €100 billion in France in 2019. As stated in *Le Monde* in 2013,

> Retail has just begun its transformation and old-style marketing is in a tizzy about it. As shopping becomes more virtual, points of sale must

supply greater experiences and sensoriality. Shops are considered essential for consumers, at least as showrooms before making a purchase on the Internet. This phenomenon affects more than just large retail chains. So-called downtown stores are also affected. These have already suffered from the construction of malls on the outskirts of cities; now, they must also compete with e-commerce, in addition to the growth of the showrooming phenomenon.[8]

More than half (54 per cent) of Europeans do it, but they are still far behind Americans (60 per cent) and Asians (71 per cent).[9]

As for anyone in the habit of buying online, any terminal can be used to access the transaction. M-commerce and s-commerce are still in their infancy. Dedicated apps constantly offer new features, through voice or video. Artificial intelligence already enables your average online shopping basket to grow. Your voice assistant will enhance your satisfaction – or will it make you spend more instead?

Although we are talking about a consumer disappointed with the system and the products offered, in this case the products are offered everywhere and incessantly, since retail, like advertising, has stressed the means instead of the content. But what is the point of this permanent availability if supply – and consequently meaning – does not keep up with it?

## Has advertising learned nothing?

If marketing's reputation is tarnished, that of advertising has been discredited even more! This makes sense, since advertising is marketing's messenger. Advertising has become the quintessential symbol of manipulation, lies, and scams. It is pure hype. And if advertisers are the heroes of successful TV sitcoms, it is detrimental to their professional image. The neurasthenic chain-smokers of *Mad Men* have no reason to envy the insidious spin doctors of political sitcoms. Advertising has become the favourite target of journalists, but it is supposedly nothing but a wrapper, an artificial structure incapable of generating meaning.

In its defence, can advertising say anything interesting about merchandise that is not real merchandise or about a promise that will not be kept? For advertising to be valuable, it must have something sensible to say. Once marketing becomes honest, it will find its *raison d'être*.

Currently, however, advertising's lack of meaning is not its sole stumbling block. The media's inevitable transformation in the face of a multiconnected World requires them to forsake their evil ways! The media are no longer content conveyors who merely exist to broadcast a pitch to their target audiences. The media must be true to their role by living up to their literal meaning. To **communicate** – where the French *communiquer* means to advertise – means to make common. That which has forever been called advertising – whose sole purpose was to render meaning public – should redeem its name and enter into a dialogue on an equal plane with its audiences.

The history of advertising with different target audiences regularly repeats a cycle in which disillusion and exuberance succeed each other with metronomic regularity. First, advertising was idolized and then it was detested and even, sometimes, both at the same time. It is difficult to appreciate this tempter, especially in times of scarcity, and it is difficult to withstand the temptation of its sirens when it promises pleasure and social connection.

In France, the advertising sector got off to a bad start. French advertising, as we know it today, was built on the doubly shaky underpinnings of nineteenth-century advertising, first, because, in France, advertising arose to pay for the cost of printing newspapers and not to drive demand for French manufacturers, which were flourishing at the time. Accordingly, advertising came into being without any need for discernment or to convey knowledge. The second reason for advertising's shaky reputation in France is that it was soon dominated by snake oil salespeople and their nefarious ilk.

Over scarcely 50 years, newspaper advertising left a bitter taste in the mouths of all those involved. It took the energy and stubbornness of a new generation at the beginning of the twentieth century to discover a new way of raising the reputation of merchandise and brands. Young professionals were well aware of the disrepute into which advertising had fallen. They proposed a new approach that involved changing the French name for advertising and it was thus changed from *réclame* to *publicité*. *Publicité* was born in 1903, but more than half a century would pass before it would begin to be considered a respectable line of business. Michelin, Citroën, LU, and L'Oréal certainly never regretted their reliance on advertising.

Advertising effortlessly adjusted to the economic growth of the 1960s and 1970s and its popularity peaked in the 1980s. At that point, pleased with itself and equipped with newfangled off-media gizmos, it changed its name again and the term *communication* replaced *publicité*. However, this step seems to have been somewhat premature because, ever since the 1990s, under its new label *communication*, advertising has been widely rejected by public opinion.

Lurching from a crisis of conscience to a crisis of trust, advertising must be wondering more than ever about its mission and its responsibilities, even if its position as an intermediary is always difficult to sustain, now perhaps even more than before.

*When in haste, disconnect your brain*

How can advertising succeed in generating constructiveness and progress when the economic crisis pressures corporations to make profits in the very short term? How can we advocate social responsibility when consumers are disoriented and often resort to parroting glib talking points? Once again, advertising is only what corporations want to make of it and what consumers are prepared to accept. The outcome of their disparate wills is unpredictable.

Thus, despite general disapproval and massive protests expressed through social media, we still often see advertising whose only discernible message is fat shaming (e.g., the emaciated models displayed by Yves Saint Laurent, Drop Dead, and Zara) or sexist (Carl's Jr., Suit Supply, Perrier, Gucci).

It is equally surprising, at a time when the issue of overconsumption is being raised all over the World, to encounter triumphal announcements of giant sales promotions, Black Friday, and monster sales. Nowadays there can be no defence for such incitement of antisocial behaviour.

Outmoded ads from the 1950s? Promotional adverts from the 1980s? No, these are contemporary advertising campaigns from all over the World in the twenty-first century: campaigns that tell us we are not grown women until we learn to select the right programme on our washing machines? Campaigns that tell us that we exist only if we overconsume? This is the upshot of one century of feminist struggle and psychoanalytical cogitation. Simone de Beauvoir and Françoise Dolto must be turning in their graves.

These examples pose real questions, each from its own particular perspective. Does advertising succeed in creating a new sort of bond? Are consumers irretrievably condemned to view old advertising clichés again and again? What does it tell us about our society when these advertising campaigns follow each other year in and year out? What does this massive bombardment bestow upon the general public? Glibness, despair, obsolescence? Long live advertising! Congratulations to its perpetrators.

## Competing to address the digital audience, a POEM in itself

As product marketing exhausts itself reinventing the wheel, advertisers are becoming puzzled about how to connect with consumers. Although there have been changes in the expectations that consumers have of products, the most pronounced change has been in media consumption, in the course of which decades of advertising culture have simply been deleted. This is because the dominant dichotomy – that between media and off media – was abolished by the growth in digital communications. In the process, all traditional yardsticks were thrown overboard. Gone are performance criteria, the good old gross rating point, or GRP, and audience measurement procedures. The financial stakes are huge and advertising professionals are overwhelmed.

This process is reflected at the terminological level. Exit the consumer. Now we speak of shoppers. No more viewing opportunities; instead we have touch points. In sum, advertisers are in a hurry to find out when and how brand names are perceived by an individual who casually switches back and forth between real and virtual lives, from the store to the tablet. Thanks to social media, everyone can now speak their mind, everybody now gets a chance to talk about brand names and consumption patterns, and Joe Sixpack gets to advertise products directly – all of which often happens beyond the control of the brand. Joël Dicker says it well:

> Marcus, just think how much a single ad slot costs in the New York City subway. A potful. People pay big bucks to display a poster with a short useful life that will be seen by only a few dozen commuters.... But now, all that is needed is to arouse interest one way or another, to create the buzz as they call it, to trigger chats about you on social media: you have access to free and unlimited advertising space. People all over the world are advertising merchandise on a global scale without even realizing it. Is that not amazing? Facebook users are just sandwich-board men who work free of charge. It would be foolish not to take advantage of their labor.[10]

Advertisers are therefore now operating in a completely different environment from before. After painstakingly structuring a profession that relied on tightly controlling the message, they are now compelled to deal with a hubbub of unscripted opinions, their own and everyone else's. Consequently, the challenge now is to dictate at what moment a brand should issue its message and when the brand is the message's subject matter. Given TV commercials, opinion blogs, mobile apps, and Twitter feeds, how is a relationship generated and who calls the tune?

We have entered the era of paid, owned, earned media, or POEM, and its cryptic interactions.

- Paid: The space I buy in the media where I paste my message.
- Owned: Media that belong to me (website, Facebook page, branded app) that I completely control.
- Earned: Every place my brand is mentioned, either unprompted or in response to my inducement (bloggers, Facebook, Twitter, and media relations are thus earned).[11]

This new structure of messages from brands or concerning them constitutes a radical change in the nature of advertising and transforms the character of advertising work. This new sort of advertising forces its practitioners to consider new manners of interaction. How can one earn a windfall? Can one spend less on traditional media? Are they obsolete? Are digital media the holy grail of brand advertising?

Top advertising agencies have concluded that to achieve optimum results, they must deploy a mix of complementary tools. Advertisers, media agencies, and consulting companies have undertaken massive investments to attempt to regain control of an ecosystem that has become enormously complex.

### *It does not matter which communication channel we use, as long as we are making sense*

A fundamental issue, however, remains. We will always be able to find a way to measure how well our tools perform, even if there are many more communication channels than before and information flows intersect and spill into each other, but what about the meaning of all this? What makes a topic interesting, regardless of its source and the medium on which it is recorded and transmitted? Finding the right path is one thing but you must also have something interesting to say. And this haste – not to say mad rush – to control communication channels detracts from core issues, such as brands, producers, and organizations of all sorts. What engrossing topic are you going to talk about to your audience? What constructive conversation can you initiate and make more appealing?

### Advertising responsibility: progress but more can be done

A few years ago, advertisers were told to start behaving responsibly. Thereupon they shamelessly usurped the argument of sustainable development. Since then, they have committed many additional blunders. Advertising and its creators have not hesitated to make grandiose and often baseless claims for the products they tout, praising their wares as natural, protective of the environment, and socially responsible. Their excesses on this score promptly boomeranged, harvesting for them rejection and mistrust, even though the underlying topic has potential to become a unifying force. The scandalous excesses of greenwashing are a case in point. Like the snake oil peddlers of old, the charlatans of advertising pounced on the ecology fad and generated a worldwide smoke screen of fatuous greenwashing ads. In this day and age, however, there is really no excuse for advertisers to exploit the environmental theme so shamelessly, for they risk once again being relegated to a purely cosmetic role and remaining the butt of media mockery. The Pinocchio Prize, for example, awarded by Friends of the Earth, lets Internet users elect "the worst liars of the year".[12]

Fortunately, thanks to the exacting and coordinated control of consumers, nongovernmental organizations, and professional organizations such as the Union of Brands (*Union des marques*)[13] and the Advertisers' Self-Regulation Agency (*Autorité de régulation professionnelle de la publicité*),[14] cases of blatant advertising malfeasance declined sharply after 2010. Consequently, our walls have ceased to be adorned with peaceful landscapes proclaiming the virtues of automobiles and petroleum products. However, the matter is not yet settled, since certain corporations persist in quibbling and the issue remains complex.

Consumers demand that brands talk clearly, transparently, and honestly. They expect brands to pay attention to their views and to furnish factual information. Consumers' opinions of manufacturers are unflattering and, according to them,

- Corporations begrudge them information on how consumer products are manufactured.
- Brands have a responsibility to change society.
- Brands possess great power to improve society's well-being.
- Brands are not always sincerely committed to sustainable development.[15]

It is frequently difficult to state one's values without being labelled an opportunist. Consumers are wary: half of them do not believe corporations that claim to be committed to sustainable development. The media churn out redundant coverage while awaiting the inevitable blunders. In the general French news media, both national and regional, the number of stories devoted to trademarks, consumption issues, responsible advertising, and eco-design grew tenfold between 2003 and 2015. Unfortunately, the media are far too prone to pounce on scoops and foster outrage, and seldom shrink from sensationalism, alarmist headlines, and overhyped TV broadcasts. Their outrage is often warranted.

In such a sensitive context, many corporations prefer to shroud themselves in silence, despite their sincere commitment and fulfilment of their corporate social responsibility (CSR).[16] Should they remain silent? Certainly not. As long as a company identifies its own strengths and weaknesses, it has everything to gain from making public any facts in its possession and declaring its commitment to well-defined and measurable goals instead of making murky and spurious claims.

No miracle recipe exists: a legitimate topic and truthful words are the minimum requirements for advertising, in addition to being interesting, creating opportunities to meet people, and fostering exchange and progress, in short, being creative or re-creative. For example, when the Optic 2000 eyeglasses chain announced its support for Yann Arthus-Bertrand's GoodPlanet Foundation and, at the same time, its intention to sell French-made frames at a promotional price, no link between these issues was readily discernible, which undermined the credibility of the brand's commitment.

### *A 2013 attempt: the sad example of Optic 2000*

On the television screen, Yann Arthus-Bertrand, perched on a tree branch and explained,

> If I film the Earth from the sky, it is merely to show you that we can all have a responsible vision to help preserve life on Earth and thus contribute to our own well-being. This is the new vision of life. Here and everywhere.

The situation is symbolic, the text convoluted, the spokesperson well known but unpopular. The pitch comes right away: "And here with our Fashion in France collection, starting at €99, Optic 2000, the leading brand in the French eyeglasses industry, is keeping jobs in France". The commercial ends by making two contradictory claims (nonsensical in itself): "Optic 2000, a new vision of life" and then "A more generous, more humane view".

The advertising campaign was murky and informed observers grumbled. Sircome, a strategic consulting company that specializes in marketing and communication remarked shortly thereafter,

> On April 22, 2013, Didier Papaz, CEO of the corporate group, was a guest at the Good Morning Business show on BFM Business radio. He said: "[Yann Arthus-Bertrand] who advocates a noble cause and speaks well of our brand, is extremely beneficial and a really nice person, and his words are full of wisdom. We will try to support him and ensure that his foundation can help underprivileged children spend their vacations on the seashore.... And I think it's a very nice gesture. The purpose of this advertising campaign is to market eyeglasses at attractive and affordable prices.... Our message is 'protect your eyes, especially when you're at the beach.' " That's all. It's hard to believe Optic 2000's account of how it fulfils its responsibilities,

since instead of launching an action programme in the field, developing it, motivating its employees, evaluating the outcome and then waiting a couple of years before going public, it simply hires an environmental celebrity with brilliant achievements to polish their image. Bingo.[17]

By contrast, when Optic 2000's competitor Atoll announced its outsourcing policy, featuring statements by its own staff, the overall impression conveyed was credible because the policy was rationally explained and the reasons stated. The corporate responsibility topic added real value to Atoll's overall brand image. Both cases involved the same industry, competing in the same market, but since they addressed the issue differently, in one case the message was sound and in the other it appeared insincere.

## Notes

1 Marie Charrel, *Le Monde*, 11 December 2014, www.lemonde.fr/economie/article/2014/12/11/les-prix-se-tassent-plus-que-ne-le-pensent-les-francais_4538269_3234.html?xtmc=supermarche&xtcr=25.

2 See www.pureagency.com/blog/324-e-la-depense-annuelle-des-francais-pour-leur-telephone-portable-1659.

3 Mathilde Damgé *Le Monde*, 14 June 2013, at www.lemonde.fr/vous/article/2013/06/14/les-francais-continuent-d-aller-a-l-hypermarche-mais-ils-n-aiment-pas-ca_3430122_3238.html.

4 M.P. McNair, "Significant trends and developments in the post war period", in A.B. Smith (editor), *Competitive Distribution in a Free, High-Level Economy and Its Implications for the University*, Pittsburgh, University of Pittsburgh Press, 1958, pp. 1–25.

5 Philippe Moati, ObSoCo (Observatoire société et consommation), at www.lobsoco.com.

6 See Alice Huot, www.ladn.eu/nouveaux-usages/etude-marketing/decathlon-michelin-leroy-merlin-quelles-marques-gagnent-la-confiance-des-francais.

7 See Amelle Nebia, e-marketing.fr/Thematique/Retail-1002/Breves/Les-franais-confirment-leur-desamour-pour-le-commerce-physique-48975.htm.

8 Showrooming (commerce) is "the practice of looking at an item of merchandise in a shop, often using a smartphone app to compare its price elsewhere, before buying it from an online distributor" (www.thefreedictionary.com/showrooming).

9 *Le Monde*, 3 July 2013, at www.lemonde.fr/economie/article/2013/07/29/la-fin-de-l-expansion-effrenee-des-drives_3454863_3234.html.

10 Joël Dicker, *La vérité sur l'affaire Harry Québert*, Editions de Falois, l'Âge d'homme, 2012, Paris.

11 See also Daniel Newman, "The role of paid owned earned media in your marketing strategy", 3 December 2014, at www.forbes.com/sites/danielnewman/2014/12/03/the-role-of-paid-owned-and-earned-media-in-your-marketing-strategy.

12 www.prix-pinocchio.org.

13 See www.uniondesmarques.fr.
14 See www.arpp-pub.org.
15 See www.influencia.net/data/document/sondage-bva-influencia.pdf.
16 The European Commission's (2011) definition of CSR (translated back from French because the English original was not available) is "companies' responsibility for the effects they have on society ...". See https://ec.europa.eu/growth/industry/corporate-social-responsibility_en.
17 See www.sircome.fr.

# 3    The emancipated consumer

A constant feature of marketing has been its effort to understand the individual. Today, study of the individual is the prime mover of challenges to the marketing industry, because understanding the individual enables marketers to grasp the rapid development of consumption toward sustainable and responsible behaviour patterns and, especially, allows them to track such development.

## Understanding the consumer: marketing's quest

Understanding the consumer is one of the basic tasks of marketing. Marketers have never given up hope of being able to model consumers in a clear and definitive manner and, at times, they have actually managed to do so. After a century of observation, we believe ourselves capable of understanding all parameters of consumer behaviour. For this purpose, we have developed very refined tools and methods of observation. Nonetheless, by dint of turning consumers into guinea pigs overfed with consumer products, marketing has paradoxically locked consumers up and put them away, perhaps in the hope of fossilizing them. A wasted effort, because consumers naturally change over time.

Change might even be the consumer's most persistent trait! The consumer is constantly changing, since he or she is first and foremost an individual located within an environment and often changes even faster than the marketing industry, which claims to possess the ultimate truths of the market and aspires to enact laws that assert its authority. Nonetheless, nowadays such efforts are far from fruitless, because they reveal how thoroughly marketers' efforts have been foiled.

Primarily by dint of appropriating the findings of the social sciences – sociology, psychology and anthropology – the marketing industry has succeeded in modelling social processes and formulating concepts, with far-reaching consequences. Today we must examine these concepts to discover whether they are capable of explaining changes in consumer behaviour.

Let us just try to see how and why. And instead of replicating antiquated models, let us use our knowledge to advance together for the common good.

## Consumer behaviour, a processing scheme

Consumer behaviour is indeed a complex process. When we try to understand the factors that drive consumers to act, react, repeat their acts, refrain from acting, and react in new ways to identical stimuli, a structure emerges that we shall call a processing scheme. It is a complex, personal procedure that each individual constructs for themself to cope with their own needs and desires. This structure can be used repeatedly, through an effort the individual only dimly discerns. The degree of this awareness is determined by the nature of the individual's initial experience.

Thus, the processing scheme is constructed according to the traits of the individual (their psyche, life story, self-confidence, tastes, and desires), depending on the nature of their bond with each social group to which they belong. Naturally, its structure is determined by the assortment of products the individual can purchase and by his or her overall environment. The scheme comprises seven successive steps: a consumer perceives a need, seeks information, then their overarching beliefs exert their influence, they compare alternative sets of desirable products, form an attitude, make the final decision, and, last, make a post-purchase assessment.

Depending on the item whose purchase is planned, only a subset of stages actually materializes. Moreover, their sequence can vary but, in general terms, we can schematically trace a path leading to the purchase. Progress along this path can be hastened or delayed by factors that can be classified into the following four domains:

- Situational factors
- Endogenous factors
- Exogenous factors
- Effects of available supply.

Let us examine these domains in greater detail to discover in what manner they might assist in encouraging responsible market behaviour.

### *Situational factors*

We have a fairly precise idea of the influence exerted on the consumer by his or her environment or habitat, especially in terms of becoming aware of environmental and economic constraints. However, to understand their impact and complete them, we must bear in mind several crucial facts (see Figure 3.1).

### The environment as a distant threat

A consumer's habitat is defined as the sum total of the biological, cultural, and political conditions that influence their consumption behaviour. Climate, traditions, and the law are probably the principal factors influencing their purchases. Despite globalization, consumption patterns still vary greatly from one part of the World to another. Exhibit A for this assertion is the widespread loyalty to local food traditions. The wearing of traditional clothing, by contrast, is unevenly distributed.

If we restrict our definition of environment to purely ecological issues, recent phenomena emerge. The media did not really start paying attention to environmental concerns until about ten years ago and, despite all the debates and controversies that have arisen, today a consensus can be said to exist.

This broad-based acceptance of the environmental dilemma seems to be a good thing; however, it poses the converse risk of being trivialized and trivialization could generate paradoxical effects. The institutionalization of crucial tasks such as sorting waste should not make us forget that the battle is not yet won. On the one hand, sustainable development is now increasingly included in these three dimensions – environmental, economic, and social. However, sustainable development can also be perceived as a secular burden, a bearer of evil news foreshadowing reprisals and crackdowns.

Environmental protection is routinely demanded by the media and civil society. Today it is our fellow citizens' third biggest worry and exerts a major influence on their consumption patterns. It is a unifying topic, but

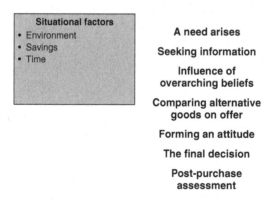

*Figure 3.1a* The consumption cycle: Step 1.

not necessarily a priority issue. People's primary consideration is for their own health and their short-term well-being, especially since the pernicious practice of greenwashing created false expectations.

Greenwashing campaigns suggest to consumers that the solutions to environmental issues have already been discovered and that applying them is just a question of time, thus easing consumers' guilty environmental consciences. Green cars, green detergents, green wrappers: "Hurray, I can simply go on consuming as before and with a clear conscience to boot!"

When consumers realized that they had been swindled, the risk of a backlash against sustainable development was substantial. The sustainable development formula can only generate progress if the government and big business agree to cooperate, even though sustainability is a fashionable buzzword incessantly declaimed in countless modulations.

So, environmental protection is an issue to which consumers are personally committed, as long as they do not feel too lonely and as long as their commitment does not cost them too much, since, after all, the crisis has already happened and the consumer's capacity for anxiety is limited.

### The economy: in the eye of the storm

The French Environment & Energy Management Agency, ADEME, is a French state-owned enterprise that implements government policies in the sectors of environmental protection and energy planning. It publishes annual opinion surveys on the French and the environment and its most recent issue shows that environmental worries in the population have declined: "Thanks to the crisis, the citizens are becoming increasingly sensitive to social issues, especially unemployment, and less sensitive to environmental issues. Pollution is only their third biggest worry, and it has now been overshadowed by concerns about social inequality". Chantal Derkenne of ADEME says, "This comes as no surprise. Whenever there's an economic slump, environmental issues yield centre stage to more pragmatic issues, principally unemployment".[1]

Therefore, we must conclude that environmental concerns recede once the initial panic subsides. Nonetheless, that is no reason to stop asking people to consume more responsibly.[2] A major argument for promoting responsible consumption is that such behaviour is likely to raise economic efficiency and can consequently help reduce the budget deficit. There can be no sensible objection to manufacturing products and providing services that, in one way or another, save endangered jobs or create new ones, especially at the local or regional level. Economic crises encourage people to concern themselves more with their immediate surroundings and to think in the short term.

*Time, a necessary but random variable*

Stephen Kerckhove states,

> In order to inhabit a social matrix, man must now be prepared to race ahead, on pain of losing on the way the core of his humanity, his ability to think and conceive of himself as a self-reliant being capable either of slowing down or speeding up.... To the delight of consumerist society, contemporary man has become a compulsive who knows nothing about himself.[3]

There can be no doubt that the phenomenon of steadily accelerating cycles influences our consumption. Social structures and economic pressures and, above all, technology have plunged us into a new space-time, the space-time of immediacy and sometimes even of ubiquity. Consumers appreciate the fact that they can order train tickets at 11 pm or do their shopping on Sunday morning without getting out of bed. Individuals who spend their time multitasking and interacting with multimedia think they can consume – or at least perform certain consumption acts – whenever they wish, since seeking information and virtual window shopping can be done at any time, regardless of international borders.

Paradoxically, this phenomenon does not imply any urgency on the consumer's part to possess the coveted good at once, because other criteria are equally important, such as the price or customization. What matters for the consumer is being able to act, for example, to search or place an order, without delay. The consumer can also patiently await the consummation of his or her purchase, namely acquiring possession or use of the merchandise, if the consumer considers the wait worthwhile. This way of stressing the present moment is merely one facet of the buying process. Finally, being able to perform certain segments of this process immediately could even be a factor that delays the final purchase – hence, the importance of very precise information on delivery times and conditions.

Minimizing wait times need not be a priority. What is essential is a defined and guaranteed deadline. Delays in delivery are generally acceptable if the item must be shipped over great distances or if customization was ordered. Longer waits are often acceptable when more than one purchaser is involved. It can take time – perhaps several days or even several months – to assemble enough purchasers for a joint purchase large enough to warrant a quantity rebate, for example.

The social phenomenon of immediacy is undeniable, but it coexists with trade-offs and bargaining of a completely individual nature.

### Endogenous factors

The second domain that influences the consumer comprises endogenous factors, which are factors specific to an individual, that is, idiosyncratic consumer traits that make that specific consumer's relationship to consumption unique. There are several such factors. They are essential to ongoing consumer developments and must therefore be borne in mind when formulating a new approach (see Figure 3.1b).

### *Attitude is a willingness to act*

Attitude can be defined as the sum total of a consumer's opinions and propensities, a state of mind that drives certain behaviour patterns. To be considered an attitude, such willingness to act must be stable and acquired. In other words, attitudes cannot be innate. Attitude is structured around three elements: the cognitive, the emotional, and the conative.

Attitude traditionally underpins an advertising process that consists in revealing, endearing, and motivating and whose effects ensue in accordance with a rational hierarchy: "I like the merchandise because of certain attributes that I perceive in it. Accordingly, and in a perfectly logical manner, I will buy it". We know today that consumers do not always abide by this hierarchy, which is flouted in the case of impulse purchases, when pressing desire overwhelms both knowledge and reason.

A crucial aspect of our process of development toward responsible consumption is its cognitive component, since it is the consumption of consciousness and consequently the consumption of knowledge. Consumers have become accustomed to ready access to an abundance of information,

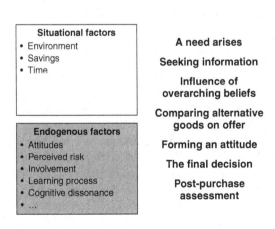

*Figure 3.1b* The consumption cycle: Step 2.

partly generated by producers but mostly conveyed by family and friends, whom the consumer considers more trustworthy then the former. Online sharing, like product recommendations via social media, affects consumer buying more strongly than price or brand and is almost as influential as word of mouth.

This constitutive element of attitude raises serious doubts concerning the role of advertising and its true effectiveness. Today brand awareness, image, and reputation emanate from multiple sources. The consumer is influenced by a hubbub of discordant voices. To find a way through a deluge of information, consumers will prefer sources they trust, primarily their peers.

### Perceived risk

Perceived risk is the consumers' (correct or false) belief that the merchandise could harm them in terms of cost (is it good idea to invest in an electric bike?), likelihood of injury (riding a bike is hazardous), difficulty of use (will I be able to ride my bike in traffic?), and social risk (what will my neighbours or my co-workers think?). However, when consumers distrust brands and businesses, it is usually because they fear for their health, their budget, or both.

Perceived risk is one of the principal obstacles to consumption. First, risk is incurred through one's routine consumption: "Can I go on eating foods containing palm oil?" "Is the paraben in my shampoo dangerous?" But perceived risk can also hamper changes in consumption patterns: "Organic food is expensive". "Car pools are such a cumbersome way to commute". Once again, it is the task of advertising to reduce the amount of risk that the consumer perceives in consuming responsibly.

### What involvement entails in unfamiliar terrain

Involvement is a measure of the interest that a consumer feels concerning a specific purchase, the importance the consumer attributes to it. It is personal and depends on the type of product, on the consumer's profile, and on perceived risk. In particular, a consumer's involvement influences how much attention the consumer pays to advertisements, how much reassurance the consumer needs, and how much information the consumer seeks.

Involvement is usually scarce for some types of products: salt, paper towels, and, for a long time, light bulbs. However, everything is reversible: the switch to energy-saving bulbs significantly changed buying behaviour. From being merchandise that aroused no interest, light bulbs have become the subject of great attention at the time of purchase. Conversely, purchases entailing a large financial investment generally generate strong involvement, such as housing, motor vehicles, and items usually bought in preparation for the birth of a family's first child. Perceived risk is high when a consumer lacks experience. Only the best will do. Immediately thereafter, involvement varies greatly from one consumer to the next, depending on the consumer's experience, interests, and concerns.

In the course of evolving toward a new consumption model, the consumer repeatedly finds themself in unfamiliar terrain. In addition, their involvement with products that they used to consider boring could increase tenfold due to a new experience. They might discover new buying methods (bartering), try new experiences (e.g., buying second-hand products), join new approaches (e.g., a co-op), distrustfully examine the objects that surround them in daily life (e.g., arrangement), or come to accept new merchandise (e.g., misshapen vegetables). Their involvement having increased tenfold, the consumer will then actively seek information and advice.

*Learning: making life more convenient*

Learning processes ensue from individual experiences (e.g. experience effect). In the course of learning, one tends either toward repetition or toward challenging what is being learned.

Upon identifying a need, the consumer builds a processing scheme of greater or lesser complexity until the purchase is consummated. The consumer then proceeds, whether consciously or otherwise, to evaluate their purchase. If their judgment is favourable, they will deem their processing scheme effective and will conclude that the experience thus acquired warrants purchasing the same item automatically if the need is felt again. Their learning process will then be complete and they will become a loyal customer. This is, of course, the expected result of any marketing approach.

If, by contrast, the post-purchase assessment yields an unsatisfactory verdict, the consumer will lose confidence in their processing scheme and, when the need is felt again, they will redesign their approach to achieve their original goals.

The concept of learning is particularly interesting when considering the changes in consumption that we have observed. Consumers who switch from one model to another are restructuring their conventional behaviour, for example by incurring risks that they believe are hazardous and by modifying the degree of their involvement with each of numerous products they habitually consume or whose consumption they envisage. Every new experience triggers a need for information, guarantees, and reassurance. Deciding to buy an electric car, for example, requires wiping the slate clean, deleting the experience of previous generations that fashioned a selection procedure to choose between a vehicle with a gasoline engine and one with a diesel engine. The boldest consumers will transform their lives even more drastically by rearranging their travel patterns to dispense with buying a car entirely!

More than ever before, consumers need information, reassurance, and motivation to make these changes and to approve of them.

### *Cognitive dissonance: a disparity that drives you forward*

An individual experiences cognitive dissonance when thinking of two things that are mutually incompatible. It is the outcome of conflict between his attitudes and his behaviour.

Cognitive dissonance causes mental discomfort and unpleasant psychological stress. Our present situation is characterized by marked cognitive dissonance. Economic crises and environmental awareness induce feelings of guilt in the consumer. Fewer and fewer consumers remain indifferent upon learning that employment in France is declining because manufacturing is being offshored to distant places, upon being told that workers risk death daily by inhaling the toxic chemicals that give our new jeans that trendy faded look, or upon reading that the shrimp on our table arrived there after travelling around the World, incinerating numerous gallons of jet fuel. After being subjected to such a barrage of cognitive dissonance, people's thinking starts changing.

Awareness of such outrages encourages behaviour patterns consistent with a sustainable development path. Regardless of whether it is experienced as a propelling force or as a new beginning, the need to act for change (motivation) will lead to a radical change in consumption requiring a switch to a satisfactory supply of products and services. This, in turn, will dispel mass anxiety, whether due to resignation, withdrawal, or rejection.

In any case, corporations that fail to prove that their output is consistent with rising expectations and with the constraints acting on the consumer will lose market share. And companies that lose market share shed jobs.

### *Exogenous factors*

A crucial domain that must be borne in mind when analysing the complex process that determines consumer behaviour comprises the effects on each consumer exerted by the various social groupings to which they belong (see Figure 3.1c). This is due to the two strands that link consumption to group identity: recognition and distinction.[4]

Our consumption is generally acknowledged to be influenced both by the tribes to which we belong and by those we wish to join. Accordingly,

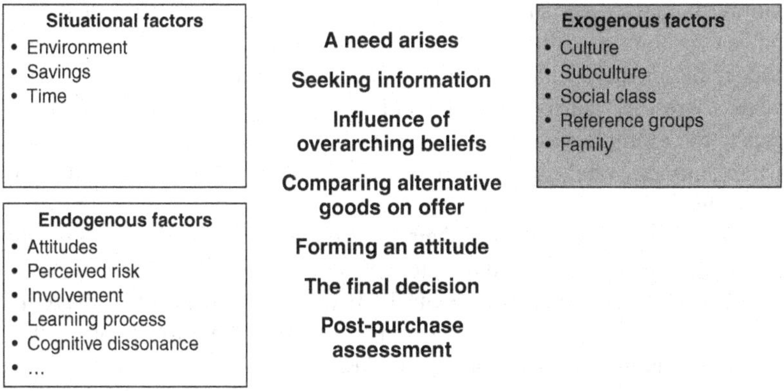

| Situational factors |
| --- |
| • Environment |
| • Savings |
| • Time |

**A need arises**

**Seeking information**

| Exogenous factors |
| --- |
| • Culture |
| • Subculture |
| • Social class |
| • Reference groups |
| • Family |

**Influence of overarching beliefs**

| Endogenous factors |
| --- |
| • Attitudes |
| • Perceived risk |
| • Involvement |
| • Learning process |
| • Cognitive dissonance |
| • ... |

**Comparing alternative goods on offer**

**Forming an attitude**

**The final decision**

**Post-purchase assessment**

*Figure 3.1c* The consumption cycle: Step 3.

we are driven by either mimicry or contrariness to make choices that label us in the eyes of our peers. Our consumption labels us as either members of our in-group or as bearers of a distinctive trait. Conspicuous ownership of prized artifacts or a preference for certain brands either nourishes the spirit of group identity or accentuates our distinctive traits. Moreover, these topics make up the bulk of all information exchanged on social media.

Facebook has grasped perfectly that proclaiming one's consumption pattern online ("liking" a certain brand) has become a component of an individual's social image. Facebook is so firmly convinced of this phenomenon that its strategy for developing so-called social commerce is based on its unrestricted exploitation. Social commerce is defined as making one's online purchases via social media, thus announcing each transaction to one's contacts in real time.

Consumers are motivated to engage in social commerce (instead of using anonymous buying options) because the in-group – the group that commands a consumer's loyalty – plays an important role in soothing consumers' anxiety and offering them advice. Sometimes an in-group even goes so far as to issue commands to its members. Moreover, in-groups act as safety nets where their members can seek refuge from any perceived risk. Remember that advice from family members invariably earns higher confidence scores than when a casual acquaintance adds their two cents.

The decision to start consuming responsibly is an implicative process that the consumer will probably be tempted to share. In all likelihood, their decision was influenced by one of their identity groups. This social and interpersonal diffusion can have an extremely powerful impact because it relies on radical individual choices that require commitment involving morality, conscience, and even civic awareness. In other words, changing one's consumption pattern is likely to involve important decisions that will trigger dissonance, which, in turn, will require additional important decisions to restore consistency. It would become psychologically complicated, for example, to decide to purchase mainly locally produced food while buying one's clothes from discounters supplied by foreign sweatshops.

A consumer who defends their choices when discussing them with others will develop persuasive arguments to convince family and friends – and also perhaps to reassure themself. If they want to join the in-group, they will have to provide evidence and make a positive effort to prove that they are making the right choices. By acting thus, the consumer will be consolidating his or her own transformation.

### *Effects of available supply*

One of the principal domains that influences the consumer is, of course, the assortment of available products and services. Exposure to merchandise or to its advertising is an essential stimulus to purchase. Whether such available merchandise seems to fulfil a need depends on its relevance and on the time, place, and conditions. We already mentioned what traditional marketing called the marketing mix, or the famous four Ps. This ideal combination was supposedly the Holy Grail for targeting consumers, which has, as we have however seen, become less effective at hitting the mark with each passing year. Because that is what the consumer really is: a target. With commendable frankness, advertisers use precisely that term. This choice of words expresses the extent to which marketing has pushed the consumer away, placing the consumer at the optimum distance for targeting.

These factors are so important to the issue that I devote an entire chapter to them. We will see that the assortment of available products and services has progressively become increasingly distant from today's consumer (see Figure 3.1d). A timeline, a context, an environment, a past experience and, of course, the perception of the available products and services – all these elements make up the consumer's many processing schemes.

## Discovering the emancipated consumer

If we follow consumer behaviour since the 1970s, say, major shifts are evident. This development of consumer behaviour can be analysed

| Situational factors | | Exogenous factors |
|---|---|---|
| • Environment<br>• Savings<br>• Time | **A need arises**<br><br>**Seeking information**<br><br>**Influence of<br>overarching beliefs** | • Culture<br>• Subculture<br>• Social class<br>• Reference groups<br>• Family |
| **Endogenous factors** | **Comparing alternative<br>goods on offer** | **Effects of available supply** |
| • Attitudes<br>• Perceived risk<br>• Involvement<br>• Learning process<br>• Cognitive dissonance<br>• ... | **Forming an attitude**<br><br>**The final decision**<br><br>**Post-purchase<br>assessment** | • Product or service<br>• Price<br>• Retail<br>• Advertising<br>• Image |

*Figure 3.1d* The consumption cycle: Step 4.

according to different criteria: the consumer's relation to consumption, expectations, morals, and dependence. We will attempt to describe the consumer's development in terms of the aforementioned criteria, first, to divide the period into successive stages of consumer development and, then, to paint a portrait of the consumer of the future.

### The emancipated consumer in detail

Consumers are no longer deceived by the economic and market system that they inhabit and do not feel indebted to it – quite the contrary, as a matter of fact. In the same way as the individual has moved away from traditional authorities such as family, politics, and the church, they no longer acknowledge this system as an infallible source of truths. On the contrary, they quite rightly think that the system has failed and that it is consequently unsatisfactory.

### The consumer is disappointed, defiant, and independent

Such disappointment after 50 years of loyalty is a disagreeable experience – a sad day after a long party. And even though the standard of well-being is higher than it has ever been, it is threatened and it endangers the planet and humanity. Promises of a better life have not been kept. Consequently, any new promise brands make will be received with scepticism. There is no more trust.

Moreover, although consumers still pay attention to marketing messages, they seldom believe them, trusting themselves first and taking

Table 3.1 The individual and consumption, 1970–2015

| | 1970 | 1990 | 2000 | 2015 |
|---|---|---|---|---|
| | Monolithic | Chameleon[5] | Consumactivist | Emancipated |
| Consumer's state of mind | Confident<br>Optimistic<br>Gullible | Self-interested<br>Well-informed<br>Fickle | Doubtful<br>Expert<br>Expectant | Disappointed<br>Mistrustful<br>Self-directed |
| Consumer's demands | Social and material progress | Personal satisfaction | Replies<br>Consideration<br>Addresses others | Personal and overall balance |
| Consumer's motivations | Progress | Benefit | Seeks meaning | Generate meaning |
| Consumer goals | More | Right now | Differently | Better |
| Consumer's expectations regarding the products and services offered | Novelty<br>Amount<br>Function<br>Product | Innovation<br>Choice<br>Convenience<br>More product | Individualization<br>Options<br>Perceived quality | Respect<br>Co-production<br>Usefulness<br>Meaning<br>Transparency |

| Consumer's expectations of the economic system | Buy<br>Build | Select<br>Take advantage | Understand<br>Find one's bearings | Approve<br>To act<br>Participate<br>Rebuild |
|---|---|---|---|---|
| Consumer's attitude within this system | Passive<br>Receptive | At ease within the system<br>Jaded | Active<br>Critical<br>Disillusioned | Able to commit, find new ways, or create more satisfying ones |
| Consumer's mode of action in this system | Conforms<br>Enthusiastic | Decodes<br>Selects | Questions<br>Challenges | Commits<br>Organizes him- or herself<br>Improvises shortcuts<br>Circumvents |
| Consumer's physical appearance | One sided | Multi-faceted<br>(court jester) | Hesitates between options<br>Schizophrenic | Rearranged<br>Complex but consistent |

Source: Touzé (2014).

the necessary steps to verify the information they need to consume knowingly and perhaps find other solutions to their needs. The consumer then broadcasts this information to their micro-implicatives (actual family and friends) or macro-implicatives (virtual family and friends, e.g. Facebook friends and followers). Thus, they could encourage others to alter their consumption patterns, perhaps enhance or besmirch a product's or brand's reputation, or inform fellow consumers of substitute products.

Cetelem, the consumer credit branch of BNP Paribas, speaks of "alternative consumers in crisis management mode",[6] consumers who prefer not to simply go on consuming and for whom consumption has ceased to be an emotional crutch. European consumers have the means to consume and to enjoy life, but they deny any particular desire to do so. A large majority of them say that they will be growing more and more concerned about environmental issues in the coming years and, in particular, that they will do their best to eat a healthy diet.

### *What does the consumer want? Personal and overall balance*

Living just to consume does not satisfy people and neither does working just to consume and consuming more and more satisfies least of all. By contrast, attaining balance between personal well-being and respect for others is a widely-shared expectation. Far from being a utopian vision, people's first experiments in consuming responsibly – particularly food – reinforce this expectation, because they have verified it for themselves. Produce that is in season, bought from a local farmer, is of better quality, more flavourful, and healthier and does not spoil as easily. Furthermore, it re-establishes a human touch while supporting local employment. On a larger scale and aside from fresh produce, French-made products have never been so persuasive and reassuring. As one experiments, this sort of consumption becomes more alluring.

### *And ultimately make sense*

The new (fair, biological, cooperative, etc.) forms of production and consumption seem likely to improve people's lives instead of promoting a mad race to the abyss. By incorporating their consumption patterns into an overall lifestyle, individuals can make commerce meaningful. This helps them shape new bonds and participate in a constructive economy. They are confident that their acts are just and reasonable. This awareness lets them reconnect being with having. They are thus free to take part in the transition from destructive to constructive consumption. For this, too, they can be proud of themselves.

Consumers are in the process of adjusting and reshuffling their consumption habits. They realize that we must scrutinize our lifestyles and consumption patterns. They are beginning to adjust gradually to a new culture of consumption that places less emphasis on possessing products and more emphasis on using them, through cooperative consumption, among other things. Thus, 35 per cent of consumers think that using a product is more important than owning it.[7]

## Living better

Responsible or alternative consumption does not necessarily mean consuming less, but it does mean consuming better: better quality, more security, more information, greater discoveries, new social links. It also provides the satisfaction of not following the herd or being controlled like a glove puppet. It means that consumption is often redesigned as a whole, but one step and one product category at a time. This transition is often an opportunity to call into question the materialistic accumulation of possessions. Consumers realize that no additional act of consumption can be justified merely because it satisfies a craving to possess more stuff. Instead, an act of consumption can only be justified through its own intrinsic meaning. Perhaps once the transition to this new consumption routine is accomplished, people will stop buying things merely from force of habit.

On the other hand, new needs will arise if they help structure overall meaning. For instance, instead of buying a new car to replace the old one, one can invest in computer equipment that is more expensive but has a longer useful life. Or one might buy a second-hand bed for the baby but choose ecodesigned feeding bottles, and so forth. The emancipated consumer has built a highly personal processing scheme for this new consumption pattern, which is in constant progress.

## The consumer wants to buy what? Respect, usefulness, transparency

Loss of trust has put a premium on respect: self-respect, respect for those who manufactured the product, respect for the environment. Consumers do not oppose innovation – quite the contrary, as long as the innovation does not insult their intelligence, their lifestyle, and the social conditions of production. And this is a cause for which consumers are willing to become involved. They are prepared to testify how they use products and their expectations of them, to participate in designing and implementing products, and to prevent and manage waste. In return, they feel entitled to know whether the supply of products and services will respect their integrity and whether it will be compatible with their decision to consume responsibly.

Accordingly, such respect must be reflected in the relationship that the consumer establishes with the brand. From the brand, the consumer will expect transparency and credible evidence that the act of consumption will be beneficial.

## *The consumer is able to make a commitment, prospect for alternatives, or devise more satisfactory arrangements*

The individual has become less dependent on the system. This demonstrates that an individual has managed to free themself from a traditional power relationship that made them dependent on the traditional manufacturer-merchant loop. Today we can fulfil most of our needs without resorting to this traditional chain. There are different ways of doing this, including purchasing directly from producers, forming a buyers' cartel to negotiate prices, or making one's own investment in product manufacturing, or else consumers can help companies or artists by buying their wares directly online or helping them via crowdfunding.

The surge in cooperative consumption is a good example of this trend. As *The Economist*[8] pointed out in 2013, this trend went from being a fringe phenomenon to the mainstream: growth in user demand makes the platforms more attractive to potential suppliers, who, by increasing supply in exchange, offer consumers more useful services. "France is becoming the world champion of this business model" and, supposedly, 52 per cent of French people have already practiced cooperative consumption, according to a recent report from the ObSoCo. "The critical mass of users does not seek any particular type of [goods or] service, but instead illustrates a mass movement that has actually made cooperative consumption one of the principal economic trends of our time".[9] ObSoCo confirmed,

> The success of the cooperative economy is not merely due to the crisis. Instead it is also based on values shared by 75% of the French people who participate in it. For 72% of respondents, cooperative practices are perceived as more respectful of the environment.[10]

These experiences reinforce a new way of thinking: you can conduct business outside the traditional model[11] and, in doing, so you can relearn how to consume. Thus, for our emancipated consumer, a purchase is no longer just an act that releases stress, but one that builds the self and integrates the consumer within a new society.

*Act, participate, rebuild*

The emancipated individual requires that both the production system and the market system be redesigned to compel them to assume responsibility and come down from their pedestals. Power relations are changing. The manufacturer and the merchant who used to dictate the rules of conduct and control all information have lost their mojo. What is expected is a genuine relationship between equals mediated through dialogue. The consumer has a role to play and takes it seriously.

Thus, when the SNCF (*Société nationale des chemins de fer français*), the state-owned French rail implicative, created the "It's up to you" website,[12] it created a community for mutual support and co-construction. In three weeks, more than 1,400 questions were asked and almost that many certified answers were received in return. A total of 84 proposals were submitted by railway passengers and two of these are currently being put into practice, as is a blog that serves as a forum to discuss how the railroad company operates and how its employees are faring.

## The consumer commits himself, organizes herself, improvises shortcuts, circumvents

Consumers have already demonstrated their ability to organize themselves when dissatisfied. Moreover, they do so by bypassing traditional systems. The various regional societies for preserving family farms (e.g. *Association pour le maintien d'une agriculture paysanne*) and the widespread consumer practice of buying from other consumers or directly from producers instead of from merchants have both become an integral part of the French landscape. In only ten years, garage sales have come into their own as venues for both business and entertainment. This is a powerful trend: as early as 2012, Harris Interactive's survey of several thousand French Internet users[13] found that, of the eight websites that ranked first in their respective business categories, three were cooperative websites.

*Consumers have grown and rearranged themselves into a complex but coherent whole*

After a period of anguish in which they were torn between their consumption patterns and their convictions and consequently suffered pangs of guilt, consumers have been seeking a new model of society that allows them to find balance and achieve consistency between their thinking and their behaviour. By learning to control their surroundings and becoming masters of their fate, they attain satisfaction and contentment, satisfaction at being not merely consumers but also human beings engaged in properly managing their social and economic lives.

This rearrangement is fragile and complex. It is fragile because it is new and because it relies on recent experiences that are sometimes disappointing. However, the generation of individuals that are now 18 to 30 years old seems to have fully appropriated these new models that it helped build. Generation Y individuals, or millennials, feel quite at ease with new functionalities and their philosophy, and are often supported by technologies that they master effortlessly, such as cooperative platforms and smartphone apps.

This rearrangement is also complex, because it is internalized in very different ways, depending on the individual. The same person might combine old habits with new behaviour patterns, depending on the situation or the type of product or service, as prescribed by that individual's own processing scheme.

### Millennials and their followers: whose turn is it to change the World?

"Young people do not respect convention", "young people use social media irresponsibly", "young people resent corporations", and so on. We have scolded Gen Y[14,15] enough. True, they antagonize their elders. And watch out, Gen Z[16,17] is coming! It seems important to point out the significant role that these generations play in the development of our economy. Additionally, these new players are not indulgent of their predecessors. They do not hesitate to reject and break off relationships that do not suit them.

Each generation transforms social conventions and appropriates the achievements of its progenitors. We must not forget that Gen Y and Gen Z were raised by their parents in the midst of economic and environmental crises compounded by incessant technological advances. In an instant, Gen Y appropriated these advances, deploying them as an idiom that enabled them to find their bearings while their elders struggle to keep up. Gen Y is the primary driver of these new models that it has managed to incorporate into a constructive vision that imposes few constraints.

It is imperative that Gen Y adapt the supply of products and services to its values and lifestyle, because, of course, it comprises the consumers of today and tomorrow. And they are independent, emancipated, and eager for new experiences.

Gen Y's and Gen Z's ostensible distaste for corporations is a sham. As citizens, they disapprove of corporations because they blame them for the headlong rush that is sweeping our economy and our environment toward an uncertain fate. As future employees, they resent rigid corporate hierarchies that evidently failed to satisfy their parents and which could fire them at the drop of a hat. Meanwhile, these same corporations incessantly strive to sell them an interminable list of gadgets and gewgaws.

Gen Y's attitude toward authority figures is marked by pragmatism. For Gen Y individuals, submission to authority is far from automatic. From their standpoint, authority is not something that one possesses but something that one emanates. To achieve acceptance, authority must prove itself. Whoever addresses them, whether a teacher, boss, or famous brand name, must start from scratch and convince them that he or she is on the level. Gen Y individuals demand evidence of expertise, evidence of quality, evidence of talent, or all three. No credit is given up front. Their trust must be earned. However, once their trust is gained, they bond seamlessly.

Accordingly, Gen Y individuals are enthusiastic about horizontal corporate structures that do not compel their loyalty arbitrarily and whose innovative output or ingenious market insertion model appeals to them spontaneously. They can become fully committed to a business model that is willing to incorporate them as full-fledged members. They can devote themselves to their tasks, organize in implicatives, and design new methods of cooperation. Their structures are nonlinear, multimodal, and multiplatform, flexible and responsive. In short, they are bursting with potential.

Whether we call them Gen Y, Gen Z, digital natives, or millennials, these generations think of the World as a seamless whole. They have inherited knowledge and worldviews from their elders and they comfortably master the technologies that enable them to deal with them. So, even though they are fully aware that the World in which they live is suffering, they are able to imagine ways to advance, to implement small solutions or large ones, gather entire tribes around an idea, and share their interests. In other words, they are able to think differently about this World. If we make the effort to put on their eyeglasses, we will discover a different view of the World, a relaxed and stimulating one, a vision that confirms for us that marketing is indeed an obsolete model.

Gen Y and, pretty soon, Gen Z will be in charge – the very people who are capable of starting an online business at age 14. And here comes generation Alpha![18]

## Notes

1  Vincent Di Grandé, *Le Monde*, 11 January 2013, *"Face à la crise, les français se détournent de l'environnement"*, at www. lemonde.fr/planete/article/2013/ 01/11/face-a-la-crise-les-francais-se-detournent-de-l-environnement_1815651_ 3244.html#d6I90uhCq9QE0Ohl.99.

2 See Sandrine Roudaut, *L'utopie mode d'emploi*, Chapter 2, Editions La mer salée, 2014, Rezé.
3 Stephen Kerckhove, *La dictature de l'immédiateté*, EditionsYves Michel, 2010, Paris.
4 P. Bourdieu, *Distinction: A Social Critique of the Judgment of Taste*, Harvard University Press, Harvard, 1984.
5 After Bernard Dubois, 1991.
6 See http://observatoirecetelem.com/les-zooms/enquete-23-responsabilite-et-ethique-dans-la-consommation.
7 www.greenflex.com/offres/produits-consommation-responsables/marketing-responsable/barometre-consommation-responsable-2019/.
8 See Martin Denoun and Geoffroy Valadon, *Posséder ou partager*, October 2013, Le Monde diplomatique, www.monde-diplomatique.fr/2013/10/DENOUN/49720.
9 ObSoCo, at www.lobsoco.com.
10 "Tous adeptes de la consommation collaborative", at http://consocollaborative.com/4575-tous-adeptes-de-leconomie-collaborative.html.
11 Cooperative Consumption, Public Service, France Inter, 2 May 2014. (Guests: Marie-Anne Dujarier, sociologist of work and organizations, lecturer at the University Paris III-Sorbonne Nouvelle, Antonin Léonard, co-founder of the Oui Share community, Anne-Sophie Novel, economist, author of *Life Share*, ed. Manifesto.
12 See http://blog.voyages-sncf.com.
13 See www.harrisinteractive.fr/news/2013/05022013.asp.
14 Those born since 1985.
15 *Le Monde*, 11 April 2014, *"Génération Y, les empêcheurs de travailler en rond"*, www.lemonde.fr/societe/article/2013/04/11/generation-y-les-empecheurs-de-travailler-en-rond_3158117_3224.html.
16 Those born since 1995, also called Generation C, which stands for communication, cooperation, connection, and creativity.
17 *Guardian*, Nosheen Iqbal, Generation Z: "We have more to do than drink and take drugs" www.theguardian.com/society/2018/jul/21/generation-z-has-different-attitudes-says-a-new-report.
18 *Guardian*, Daniel Lavelle, "Move over, millennials and Gen Z – here comes Generation Alpha" www.theguardian.com/society/shortcuts/2019/jan/04/move-over-millennials-and-gen-z-here-comes-generation-alpha.

# 4    The brand

## Friend or foe?

*Nowadays the fundamental trait of brands must be honesty. A brand can have flaws but it must be sincere and must make efforts to improve itself, as well as explain how it is doing so.*

A brand sums up a company's competencies and epitomizes its values. By investing in its brand, a company makes it part of its history and the brand eventually comes to symbolize the company itself. The brand has become the very image of a company, the spearhead of its acts and values. According to the World Intellectual Property Organization,[1] "A trademark is a sign capable of distinguishing the products or services of one enterprise from those of other enterprises". However, a trademark is actually much more. Brands began as a form of legal protection, but economists say that a company's brand today has become one of its most valuable assets. (Its value can be staggering: up to 80 per cent of the market capitalization of corporations such as Nike and Chanel.) More than a list of items or a number at the bottom of a balance sheet, a brand is a combination of materials, symbols, acts, and interactions.

However, this symbol, conceived to differentiate and establish bonds, is undergoing an unprecedented crisis. That is because consumers, under the influence of economic constraints and inspired by new ideals, are having trouble bonding to brands. Consumers may want brands, but the new hopes that they place in them are often dashed. Even worse, consumers question brands' sincerity, even – and perhaps most of all – that of the largest brands.

The fundamental characteristic of today's brand is honesty. A brand can be imperfect, but it must be sincere and make an effort to improve. A brand must also explain what it is doing to improve itself.

## Mistrust at all levels

Whereas brand names may originally have been considered safe havens in troubled times, in this case their effect has been merely to foster doubt. This paradoxical outcome of a failed relationship is yet another sign that marketing has reached the end of its tether – constantly offering more until all relevance and attractiveness has been lost, constantly saying more, only to wind up becoming inconsistent.

The development of the relationship between brand and consumer is similarly fraught with doubt. What do consumers think of brands? What do they expect of brands? Their attitudes change from year to year. For example, in its 1994 and 2010 consumer surveys, the Research Center on Living Conditions (*Centre de recherche pour l'étude et l'observation des conditions de vie*, or CREDOC) polling organization asked French consumers, "What do you consider a good brand?" The answers reflect the growth in consumer expectations over 16 years. Specifically, consumers increasingly expected a brand name to offer an assurance of making the right choices. Brands began as markers of social status and later came to stand for quality products. Currently, priorities focus on steadily increasing the component of rational reassurance that brand names offer consumers.

Our degree of technological progress and standardization today should ensure that any product on the market fulfils at least minimum quality standards. That should be the least of our concerns. However, recent scandals in the food and textile sectors have shown that such assumptions regarding quality were somewhat precarious, even for so-called top brands. Whereas criteria such as ruggedness and durability were virtually absent in 1994, 16 years later they made up 13 per cent of the attributes volunteered by consumers when describing a "reliable brand". Furthermore, that time-span witnessed a fourfold increase in consumer mentions of a link between brand name and corporate responsibility.

From a rational standpoint, brands should primarily prevent consumers from buying the wrong item; however, what they really do instead is encourage consumers to assert their identity and identify themselves through the parameters of pleasure, convenience, stylishness, and novelty.

Brands are supposed to instil trust but, instead, widespread scepticism of merchandise has been followed by a growing wariness of brands themselves! Without exception, marketing studies show a paradoxical tension in consumer attitudes toward brands, wavering between attraction and desire, frustration and apprehensiveness. Whereas, on the one hand, brands are valued for their ability to innovate and for the pleasure they give consumers, by contrast, their ability to reassure is meagre indeed. Their function is to send a signal and to offer a guarantee.

When TNS Sofres conducted its tenth survey on advertising and society in October 2013, asking respondents to grade the top brands of staple products according to various attributes, the attribute that ranked the lowest was a brand's ability to reassure.[2] Additionally,

> In the context of a trend toward growing wariness of big business (a drop of 28 points compared to 2004, 29% confidence in 2014) and substantial but waning scepticism toward brand commitment (49% expressed mistrust of product information furnished by manufacturers of durable products, a drop of 4% compared to 2010), French consumers said they wanted a guarantee that products are of good quality and do not impair their health.[3]

CREDOC[4] confirms that, among purchasing criteria, trust in brands has been declining since 2000. The longer a consumer has been purchasing a brand, the warier of it the consumer becomes. As the consumer becomes more self-assured, trust in brands declines. Advertising is deemed ineffectual and its power to persuade has diminished. Consequently, when brands resort to greenwashing, their claims carry little weight and charges of opportunism are promptly raised.

Brands are permanent transmitters of signals. The mere existence of a brand and its availability on the market make it a source of signals and meaning. A brand can be displayed to consumers in many different ways and at any time, for instance, whenever a brand is advertised or seen on the wrapper of a staple good sold in a store, whenever a consumer is seen by her family and friends using a branded product, and whenever a brand is mentioned in a news story or recommended by consumers via social media. This multifarious and overlapping signalling makes it difficult to ensure message consistency. The falsehood of Nestlé's chocolate cake mix clashes with its pretensions to responsible supply chain management. Consumers are not taken in, because this is precisely the sort of deception they are most likely to resent.

The advertising slogan "Major brands are committed" thus scarcely inspires consumer confidence.

Note how this advertising campaign by Prodimarques[5] (a syndicate of 70 French corporations that manufacture major brand consumer products) promotes 15 major national and multinational brands by asserting their common commitment to social and environmental policies:

> In a world where everyone seems to care only for himself, it is major brands that step in to bring joy to the most vulnerable kids, it is the

major brands that day in, day out help us enjoy life, it's the major brands that help us share unforgettable gourmet dishes. Today major brands are committed to the future.

However, a common language is out of the question when not all of these brands are committed to the same goals or when they are not all committed to the same degree. Admittedly, specific information provided online fills in the gaps left by generic TV commercials. Such information enables elaborations on broad policy statements by furnishing specific facts intended to corroborate them. But once again, the inconsistency of the facts precludes credible proof. Does the fact that 98 per cent of a certain cheese consists of milk demonstrate any particular sense of responsibility?

## Points of reference and contracts

Blot, scar, emblem, grade, hallmark, identification marker, label, logo, mark, marker, proprietary name, *quality, sign, slur, smirch, sort, species, stain, stamp, symbol, taint, trademark, trade name, type,* and *variety* are some of the 36 synonyms of the word *brand* in *Collins' English Thesaurus.* Among these synonyms, we find the dimensions of a concept more complex than initially meets the eye. The term comes from Middle English

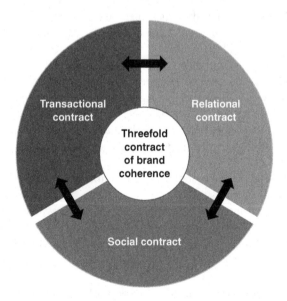

*Figure 4.1* Threefold contract of brand coherence.

*brand*, which meant torch and is derived, in turn, from the Old English *beornan* or *byrnan*, to burn (*American Heritage Dictionary*, 5th edition). George Lewi and David Aaker[6] construe brand as a mental reference point. These different approaches highlight the complexity of the concept and its challenges. Beyond a name or a logo, to understand what is at stake in a brand, we must remember that the core of a commercial transaction is the link between buyer and seller.

Furthermore, a brand stands primarily for an implicit contract entered into with its purchasers. This contract constitutes the justification for choosing one brand over a different one. In this contract, three major aspects can be distinguished: a transactional contract that reduces the uncertainty of the purchase and provides a concrete, tangible response to a need or desire; a relational contract that enables a relationship to be established, developing values and a shared experience; and a social contract that endows consumption with meaning by referring to societal values. Unless all three contracts are both proposed and fulfilled, the brand will undermine the basis of the relationship.

What counts is not what a brand says about itself, but how it performs. Consider the following two examples.

Whereas Apple used to be considered an exemplary model and was considered *the* brand *par excellence*, having managed to reconcile product quality, desirability, and shared ideas, eventually its gritty industrial reality caught up with it. Apple may be no worse than its competitors, but its competitors did not promise us the moral standards of a new epoch. This made the revelation of its sordid industrial practices all the more shocking.

*Table 4.1* The dissonance inherent in Apple's threefold contract

| | | |
|---|---|---|
| Transactional contract | +++ | New product, product quality, new uses |
| Relational contract | +++ | Pleasure, styling, its vision of the world and of the industry |
| Social contract | —- | Actual employee working conditions, closed-circuit system |

*Table 4.2* The dissonance inherent in Nutella's threefold contract

| | | |
|---|---|---|
| Transactional contract | +++ /—- - | Inimitable taste/nutritional hazard |
| Relational contract | +++ /—- | Pleasure, tradition, family firm/lack of transparency |
| Social contract | —- | Supply chain severely damages the environment |

Nutella hit the jackpot on the strength of its unique flavour. It became the emblem for a greedy childhood, a cult brand revered by its consumers. But what about products that invoke cherished childhood memories but are also likely health hazards or whose production entails laying waste to vast forests?

In the case of these two examples of contracts containing internal contradictions, their inconsistency has not harmed their sales. Consumer awareness and media coverage of these issues, however, damaged these brands, which nonetheless remain extremely popular. This breach of the contract binding the brand to the consumer leaves a bitter aftertaste or an uneasy conscience and is likely to ease the market entry of more persuasive competitors.

Hence, it is important for a brand to be very firmly grounded in its principles so it can enunciate an unambiguous contract and then fulfil it. A brand must not deviate from its course and must avoid at all costs any temptation to feign commitment. It will naturally be better for it to refrain from any acts or behaviour patterns inconsistent with its stated policy.

## Flawed perhaps, but honest

Yup, it's tough being a credible brand nowadays, certainly much more so than previously, because consumers are raising new demands that are difficult to reconcile with the state of industry. As shown by the Cetelem Observatory, consumers who first of all select a brand based on the favourable quality-to-price ratio of its products (72 per cent) also claim that their choice depends on criteria such as supporting employment in the country where they live (61 per cent), defence of the environment (58 per cent), being informed about raw materials and manufacturing processes (56 per cent), and a commitment to health (50 per cent). In addition, they see themselves as true partners of brands, offering to test merchandise before it is placed on the market (70 per cent).

Consumers make rational decisions when deciding how to improve their consumption patterns: one-fourth say they prefer local firms and one-third say they take care to avoid buying products made by firms of whose behaviour they disapprove. A total of 80 per cent of them say they do not receive enough information on the manufacturing conditions of products.[7] Consuming responsibly means first and foremost consuming differently (well-labelled products, ethical certificates, local production, less pollution).[8]

To fulfil these requirements, brands must be redesigned from scratch. Brand names must again represent a guarantee. Those that fail to do so are devoid of meaning. In addition, such a guarantee must cover more than just a product's inherent quality; it must also cover the source of its inputs, its production conditions, and its manufacturing processes.

But I am getting ahead of myself. Consumers do not require everything right away. They are quite capable of understanding the inertia of an industrial organization, the complexity of globalized production, and their underlying reasons. By seeking the lowest price, they bear some of the responsibility for this state of affairs.

## The brand, open 24/7

"Brands are developing in the minefield of objectivity and of universally accessible information".[9]

Consumer demands determine all aspects of a brand's business efforts. Since brands are now permanently accessible, the relationship must be consistent not only from place to place, but also at all points in time.

A brand must manage a relationship that is renewed with each encounter. Since brands now exist online, encounters occur hundreds of times more often than they did before the advent of the Internet. Moreover, these encounters do not consist merely of consumers being exposed to advertisements. In addition to advertising, they comprise the creation of bonds, conversations, and purchases. Today brands never shut down, which multiplies both the opportunities and risks, since brands now control neither the message nor the retail establishments where they are sold. Their consumers talk about them, their merchants talk on their behalf, and their critics trash-talk them. The chimera of ubiquity is attained, together with its myriad risks.

Although this ubiquity bodes well for future business growth, this promise will only yield fruit if companies rely on a perfectly sound, sincere, and controlled triad, as shown in Figure 4.2.

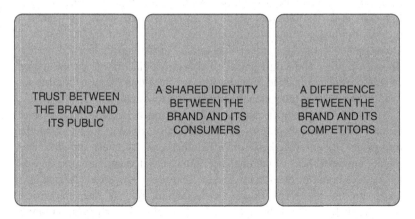

*Figure 4.2* The three strong brand's pillars.

## Defending one's name to defend one's acts

Given this situation, is it still meaningful to distinguish between product brand and company brand?

At a time when being informed about the source of raw materials and the soundness of manufacturing processes is paramount and when these will eventually be revealed anyway, a brand is a particularly attractive base on which companies can rely. It is a signal and a guarantee.

A company that seeks to instil trust does not benefit from hiding behind a maze of different names. Instead, it should be transparent and own up to its responsibility for the products and services it supplies. Instead, however, everywhere we see clusters of brand names piled higgledy-piggledy on top of each other. This is the phenomenon called brand architecture: successive tiers of brands built for marketing convenience that ultimately do nothing but alienate the consumer.

Oh, you're eating a Mikado King Choco? That belongs to the Mikado brand. Mikado chocolates are made by LU baked products. But we have not reached the top of the pyramid yet, because LU belongs to Mondelez.

Oh, you're making Milky Soft instant mashed potatoes? Milky Soft belongs to the Maggi line of instant mashed potatoes. What about Maggi? Maggi is a brand of prepared foods. Maggi belongs to Nestlé.

Is all this really necessary? Brand architecture is expensive for companies. This structure may have fulfilled consumer expectations at one time or another but, nowadays, with such labyrinthine ownership structures being a menace to society, is this model still sound? Admittedly, none of this information is secret and each corporation clearly designates its various brands but, in such a situation, consistency becomes an illusion.

Take the Dove brand name as an example. By announcing itself as the brand of toiletries that sees beauty in every woman, Dove has signed a morally binding contract with its customers. All women are beautiful and Dove is their everyday partner – to attain simple and unadorned beauty, devoid of glitter and sexist games of seduction, elaborating on the notion of self-assurance regained, a brand-new realm within the mass market for beauty, particularly relevant and universally acclaimed.

However, it so happens that the Dove brand belongs to the Unilever Group, which few consumers have ever heard of, since its logo lurks in the fine print. Unilever markets some 30 other brands. These include completely unrelated lines of merchandise, such as Lipton and Snuggle, as well as the Axe brand of deodorants and men's toiletries, whose advertising is based on the archetype of macho seduction, that is, the diametrical opposite of Dove. Even though Axe's advertising is humorous, and even derisive, the yawning gap that separates these two Unilever brands means the corporation is sending consumers two completely inconsistent messages. Will the real corporation please stand up?

How can I trust a corporation that, in its Dove persona, tells me to trust myself and my choices? Which is the real Unilever? Why is Unilever talking out of both sides of its mouth? The flagrant contradiction of its messages fills me with misgivings. The overall impression is one of discordance.

Unilever has become aware of its own paradoxes. After having changed the discourse of the Axe brand towards male passions and inspirations, the entire company, through the voice of its new manager, is announcing a radical shift: Unilever has warned it will sell off brands that do not contribute positively to society. In July 2019, Alan Jope asked: "Can these brands figure out how to make society or the planet better in a way that lasts for decades?" (Make society or the planet better: these capacities would become, for the manager, the rationale for being indispensable in today's brands (their purpose). His comments raised the possibility of the company selling off profitable brands, potentially hurting the bottom line, but Jope said: "Principles are only principles if they cost you something".[10]

Of course, such disorderly marketing architectures are the outcome of many decades of development, investment, and corporate buyouts and divestments. Admittedly, this profusion of brands was cultivated to please the consumer. No effort was spared to create watertight compartments, decontaminated of any association, and to conceal the fact that a brand created by a middling domestic firm had been bought out by a faceless multinational juggernaut.

Today, in a great explosion of transparency, corporations are backtracking and instead displaying their portfolio's size and sometimes its intricacy. How does all this concern today's consumer? The financier, the investor, the shareholder, sure, this is understandable, but how about the consumer? What benefit do consumers derive from the fact that their staple products – their private consumption – comprise a tangle of hieroglyphs that they now know is nothing but a front? This is an additional explanation for the loss of trust.

If a company markets a broad range of products, it can signal its commitment through a short, simple backup brand, which would enable unfettered portfolio management. To establish the transparent consumer relationship that is so essential, a brand must present itself as a distinct and coherent whole

The stakes are high in a financial market environment where corporate buyouts are the name of the game. What will those brands be worth once they definitively forfeit the trust placed in them?

Japanese brands have been particularly successful at simultaneously conducting numerous disparate lines of business. People seem untroubled by the simultaneous availability on the market of Yamaha guitars and Yamaha motorcycles. Pruning and simplifying portfolios would permit Yamaha to restore a relationship, which would save time and capital investment and would enlighten and ultimately soothe the anxiety of public opinion.

A company must be able to defend its name to defend its actions. If the company is not perfect or if the multiplicity of its lines of business is likely to foster inconsistency, it can simply say so and explain why. There is no reason why consumers cannot listen to the company's explanation and judge for themselves. But it has become crucial for the contract to be unequivocal.

Orange made that decision when it dropped its old corporate name, France Télécom, in order to speak with a single voice, and that is what it told the public, in so many words. In a letter to its shareholders on 15 July 2013, Orange stated,

> This change results from a decision that reflects the values of a French corporation proud of its roots, its achievements and its history. Lastly, this change gives us an opportunity to address the public once again and reassert our role and our mission.

So, yes, corporations will have to own up to all their acts, products, and management methods, since it is a coherent whole and not merely a commercial brand that, on the one hand, sells stylish products and, on the other, makes profits by exploiting the World's social ills. Corporations must speak with a single voice for unconditional commitment. To top it off, I know exactly what I am consuming when I choose Orange.

## Branding: far too serious a matter to leave to marketing pros

If the concept of brand has become so important, it is because merchandise no longer consists of just a set of functional traits but has, instead, become a way to create meaning. Nobody can absorb the flood of information that is now only a mouse click away. Where can we find meaning? In the brand.

A product is a commodity made in a factory. A brand, by contrast, is a value bought by a human being. A product can be copied by a competitor. A brand, by contrast, is unique. A product has an expiration date. A brand, by contrast, is meant to endure.

More than ever before, a brand can signal to the public the sincere commitment of the company that owns it. And that is far from all. Far more than the mere utility of a manufactured artifact, a brand expresses the character of the entire company; it announces its mission and the justification for its existence.

Let us leave marketing aside for a moment and take a panoramic look at the corporation.

### Everything an entire company entails

A brand is consequently witness to a finely attuned bundle of diverse energies: the leadership and vision of a management board or a creator and the ability to innovate, organize people, make purchases, and assure quality (see Figure 4.3). Finally, a brand is a firm's bond with the public. A brand's success is the outcome of a consistent overall project that is clearly articulated for the consumer's benefit: proper positioning.

Brand positioning results from a strategic decision intended to fashion the image the company seeks to instil in its public's mind. This notion reminds us that the market resides not only in store display cases but also primarily in consumers' minds. Consumers have lost their trust in brands because brand positioning is no longer suitable or lacks crucial

*Figure 4.3* Overall value of a brand.

components. Additionally, as we see today, it lacks consistency, because for far too long corporations focused on product positioning, whereas they must now think in terms of brand positioning, which can only be done by, first, acknowledging that consumers are becoming emancipated and, second, considering the sum total of a corporation's behaviour.

### Brands' consistency and durability

Are a brand's mission and commitment to its goals unequivocal? Are they shared with the corporation's staff and subcontractors?

The brand must be a custodian of authenticity. Does the corporate structure encourage the fulfilment of the brand's commitments? How can we make sure that the mishmash of messages conveyed by the corporation's various lines of business do not clash with each other? Research and development, design, procurement, production, finance, advertising – all segments of the enterprise must be devoted to the same mission.

Has a charter been drawn up explaining the brand's mission and values and how they should be presented? Has anyone in particular been hired as the Temple Guardian? The brand manager should be the chief executive officer or, failing that, another top executive. And it should be obvious that this executive has largely stopped handling marketing issues!

Only by defining the brand with the greatest precision and by structuring the company cross-functionally can the reciprocal consistency of the three contracts implicit in a brand be assured: namely, its relational contract, its transactional contract, and its social contract.

### Company contracts

Le Bon Coin's mousy little website promptly trounced other marketing colossuses such as eBay. Without ever ceasing to be modest and user-friendly, while keeping all its promises, it fulfils a need. Its management conforms to type – pragmatic, unassuming. Its staff turnover is the lowest among a ranking of new technologies and this French company is as profitable as US market leaders!

*Table 4.3* The coherence of Le Bon Coin's (France's equivalent to Craigslist) threefold contract

| | | |
|---|---|---|
| Transactional contract | +++ | Simple, accessible, free of charge |
| Relational contract | +++ | Modest, friendly |
| Social contract | +++ | Creates bonds, subdued style, refrains from ostentation |

*Table 4.4* The coherence of Weleda's threefold contract

| | | |
|---|---|---|
| Transactional contract | +++ | Product quality, high-quality raw materials, fun to use |
| Relational contract | +++ | Attaining beauty and health by respecting nature and trusting people |
| Social contract | +++ | Demonstrated environmental management and social commitment |

Weleda never deviated from its original course – set out by its founder, Rudolf Steiner, in 1920 – unconcerned by short-lived fads in the cosmetics market. The company has sprouted a variety of product lines, from cosmetics to medicine, all in keeping with the mission it set for itself: high-quality natural input and respect for people and for nature. Weleda France has invested in a new eco-designed building that will double its manufacturing capacity over the next 15 years. Founded in Switzerland, the corporation now has branches in 50 countries on every inhabited continent.

Bel'M is the biggest European manufacturer of front doors for houses. The company has devoted great effort to research and development in materials science. It has succeeded in growing for the last 25 years thanks to its skill at meeting consumer expectations while becoming more committed to social and environmental issues each year.

It is immediately clear that this branding is far more capable of inspiring commitment than the old, worn-out kind of marketing, provided, that is, that we do not seek meaning where there is none. Instead, we must fulfil a mission that really does exist. The brand can become the symbolic crucible of a company's overall responsibility and can convey a message far more substantial than a mere advertising campaign or product information.

All acts performed by a company and/or brand contribute to this crucible and enrich its output, that is, its products or services, its behaviour, its policies, and its attitude. The company's ability to create trust and bonds with the emancipated consumer will result from its ability to understand

*Table 4.5* The coherence of the Bel'M threefold contract

| | | |
|---|---|---|
| Transactional contract | +++ | Creativeness, innovation, sustainability, performance |
| Relational contract | +++ | Custom-made products, trust, transparency |
| Social contract | +++ | Active commitment to CSR, French made, pilot company for environmental labelling |

and respect the consumer through a comprehensive approach and by optimizing an entire supply chain.

The brand is a mission, a positioning, a commitment – and countless opportunities!

## Notes

1 See www.wipo.int/trademarks/en/index.html.
2 *Publicité et Société*, TNS SOFRES-Australie, "*2004–2013, c'était le future*", at www.tns-sofres.com/sites/default/files/2013.10.17-pub.pdf.
3 www.greenflex.com/offres/produits-consommation-responsables/marketing-responsable/barometre-consommation-responsable-2019/.
4 See www.credoc.fr.
5 See www.prodimarques.com.
6 G. Lewi and J. Lacœuilhe, *Branding Management*, Pearson Education, Paris, 2016.
7 https://info.greenflex.com/contenu-barometre-greenflex-consommation-responsable-2019.
8 https://info.greenflex.com/contenu-barometre-greenflex-consommation-responsable-2019.
9 Olivier Bronner, president of Plan.Net. *E-marketing*, 1 March 2011, "*Consommation: le nouveau statut de la liberté*," at www.e-marketing.fr/Marketing-Magazine/Article/Consommation-le-nouveau-statut-de-la-Liberte-39114-1.htm.
10 *Guardian*, Zoe Wood, 25 July 2019 "Unilever warns it will sell off brands that hurt the planet or society" www.theguardian.com/business/2019/jul/25/unilever-warns-it-will-sell-off-brands-that-hurt-the-planet-or-society.

# 5 Implicative marketing

> Imagine a sort of marketing that is pragmatic, constructive, and capable of satisfying new human desires, a sort of marketing that is sustainable and creates value for corporations.

The first four chapters have described how a worn-out system is facing the abyss and why we must envisage a different sort of marketing altogether. Nonetheless, if we were to redefine marketing, perhaps we would not be so far from its original formulation: to promote the sale of products by fulfilling consumer expectations to the best of our ability. This definition is perfectly consistent with the reform of marketing I propose here, which seeks to establish a mutually satisfactory bond between consumers and businesses. At the same time, it is the diametrical opposite of sclerotic conventional marketing in terms of outcome, approach, and historical context.

## Implicative marketing enables new angles of approach

Accordingly, it is time to devise a type of marketing adapted to a new historical period and to take the liberty of scrutinizing the rules from a new angle. We start with a classic in the field, namely, Abraham Maslow's[1] celebrated hierarchy of needs theory, embodied in Maslow's pyramid.

Maslow's pyramid (see Figure 5.1) has been guiding marketing thinking since 1943. It consists in a sequential logic of the needs felt by humans. In its original, or simplified, form, it postulated that human needs arise in a certain sequence and that a need begins to be felt only once the need immediately preceding it has been satisfied. The two bottom levels, or stages, comprise primary needs that can be summed up under the concept of having, that is, the sum of one's possessions. The three upper levels comprise secondary needs that constitute social being. Maslow's pyramid

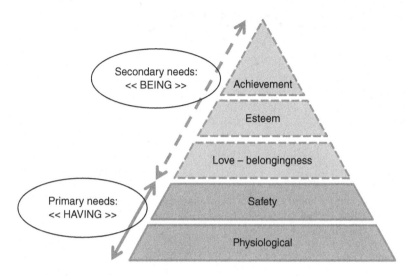

*Figure 5.1* Maslow's hierarchy of needs.

accurately depicts the manner in which consumption's position in society has developed since the 1950s. During that period, once physical comfort had been attained, consumption swiftly switched to social comfort.

In marketing circles, Maslow is a touchstone, reflecting a consensus, something reassuring and unquestioned. In our turbulent process of evolution toward responsible consumption, however, in the course of which marketing is daily vilified and called into question, what does this pyramid mean to us?

Just a few years ago, we thought that responsible consumption responded principally to a need for self-actualization on the part of a privileged few who had reached the topmost stratum of society. Since then, though, we have discovered that responsible consumption is actually an ideal cherished by people from all walks of life.

Consuming responsibly is not the attainment of privileged elites but, instead, a need that is in the process of becoming a central value in society that must underlie individual commitment. This makes us descend within the pyramid! More precisely, this will lead us to reconsider the pyramid, because the hierarchy that Maslow proposed in 1943 is outmoded. Given economic crises and new yearnings, any transition from one stage to the next is dubious.

For the first time in 50 years, people are wondering about what has been achieved. Satisfaction of our primary needs might not be assured for much longer, given energy crises, water pollution, economic injustice, and waste. Physiological and safety needs are again centre stage for the bulk of the World's population! Could an inversion of the pyramid be relevant? The reality is more complex, because having and being intersect or collide: "Yes, I would like to drink water from a nice designer bottle, but it must be water without phosphates or bisphenol and it must have been shipped without generating any waste or greenhouse gases".

The five levels of need are indeed connected to each other, but not just in terms of contiguity. Each level is connected not only to the levels immediately above and beneath, but to [all?] other levels as well. As a matter of fact, each type of need is related to all the others. Moreover, the originally postulated linear sequence of levels is actually fictitious. Thus, by crossing the links instead of merely listing them sequentially, we would begin thinking and functioning in a manner much more consistent with that of contemporary consumers:

- "I will be able to ensure my safety through my group identity" (i.e., belonging and love in Maslow's model). "By belonging to the group, I form part of an implicative that protects me and to which I am committed" (local consumption, co-ops, family farm preservation, etc.).
- "I will learn self-esteem – and learn to appreciate others – by satisfying my vital needs in a responsible fashion" (organic and fair consumption, etc.).

This cross-connectedness means that the spheres of being and having are no longer separate; instead it binds them together. Sociology taught us that consumption enabled social existence and we were led to believe in the logic of "I am because I possess". Nowadays – and this is where the pyramid is transformed – we can assume that consumption is also obtained through existing in society: "I possess because I am". This second logic does not replace the previous one but, instead, intertwines with it by giving the process a new layout.

Consequently, we propose a new vision of the consumer, literally a revolution, (see Figure 5.2) that is, the transition from a vertical and linear logic to a cross-functional and interrelational approach. This does not simplify the marketer's task but it does permit the adoption of new principles with which to reconnect with contemporary consumers, who have very little resemblance to the consumers of the 1950s and 1960s.

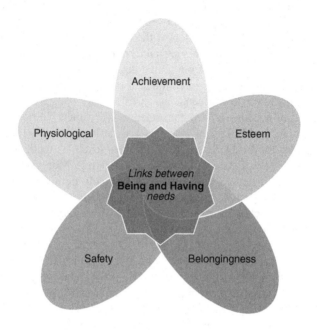

*Figure 5.2* Interlinking needs: the Needs Daisy.

## Implicative marketing: listening to the emancipated consumer

To achieve the transition from a consumer society that depends on destructive marketing to a society that co-produces a sort of marketing capable of building shared and sustainable progress, we can identify a set of specific pathways, that is, new approaches, to developing a marketing strategy that listens to consumers, supports their motivations, and propels a new kind of consumption.

Our starting point for structuring this new approach is the theory of basic human values propounded by Shalom Schwartz.[2] Schwartz, a psychologist, proposed a theory that lists and orders eleven values: self-direction, stimulation, hedonism, achievement, power, security, conformity, tradition, benevolence, universalism, and spirituality. To serve our goals, emancipated consumers can construe these values to suit their tastes and then define the tasks that should be entrusted to implicative marketing.

## 1. Self-direction

Independent thought and action: choosing, creating, exploring.

**Expectations of the emancipated consumer:** Has become independent of the market system or wishes to.

**The mission of implicative marketing:** Respect people's self-direction. Gain the consumer's loyalty by virtue of the consumer's own decision instead of by constantly amassing consumer data.

## 2. Stimulation

Excitement, novelty, and challenge in life.

**Expectations of the emancipated consumer:** Yearns for new experiences, wants to unclutter his life, and wishes he were bold enough to start living a different kind of life.

**The mission of implicative marketing:** Offer a responsible assortment of products.

## 3. Hedonism

Pleasure or sensuous gratification for oneself.

**Expectations of the emancipated consumer:** A pleasant life is consistent with the values of simplicity, truth, true quality, restraint, and rediscovering healthy consumption.

**The mission of implicative marketing:** Guarantee quality, ethical sourcing, and sustainability.

## 4. Achievement, success

Personal success by demonstrating competence in accordance with social standards.

**Expectations of the emancipated consumer:** Making one's acts meaningful, being conscientious.

**The mission of implicative marketing:** Make a commitment, report on suppliers' honest and sincere behaviour.

## 5. Power

Social status and prestige, control or dominance over people and resources.

**Expectations of the emancipated consumer:** Making his or her dealings with others meaningful, setting an example, being innovative.

**The mission of implicative marketing:** Re-empowering consumers, letting them control things (by reusing them or using them in new ways).

## 6. Security

Safety, harmony, and stability of society, of relationships, and of self.

**Expectations of the emancipated consumer:** Controlling the quality of what one consumes, making consumption safe for oneself and for the environment.

**The mission of implicative marketing:** Warranty, traceability, control of the supply chain, precautionary principle.

## 7. Conformity

Restraint in one's acts, inclinations, and impulses likely to upset or harm others and violate social expectations or norms.

**Expectations of the emancipated consumer:** Taking part in a constructive trend.

**The mission of implicative marketing:** Informing, promoting the progress achieved, demonstrating.

## 8. Tradition

Respect, commitment, and acceptance of the customs and ideas one's culture or religion provides.

**Expectations of the emancipated consumer:** Relying on long-term common sense.

**The mission of implicative marketing:** Referring to the social and cultural context and being modest.

## 9. Benevolence

Preserving and enhancing the welfare of those with whom one is in frequent personal contact (i.e., in-group).

**Expectations of the emancipated consumer:** Sharing, social bonds.

**The mission of implicative marketing:** Respecting the individual, co-production, relationships, encouraging community spirit.

## 10. Universalism

Understanding, appreciation, tolerance, and protection of the welfare of all people and nature.

**Expectations of the emancipated consumer:** Respect for human rights, respect for communities, resources, and the environment.

**The mission of implicative marketing:** Responsible control of the supply chain, fair trade, reducing environmental impact.

## 11. Spirituality

Meaning, consistency, inner harmony.

**Expectations of the emancipated consumer:** To be soothed.

**The mission of implicative marketing:** Respect, simplify, guide, support, refrain from encroaching.

By working on these eleven angles, a company can identify, for each of its projects, whether it actually complies with one or more values of emancipated consumers. The company can then decide how it will nurture and develop a new bond with its public.

## Implicative marketing: the new company mediator

The mere application of new tools of analysis will not suffice to impel the changeover from conventional to implicative marketing. Such a merely technical approach will just affect appearances. To fulfil its new missions, marketing must insert itself into a new niche in the firm: that of mediator and "involver". Consequently, it must link directly to the company's various departments and – why not? – be fully incorporated within the firm. That is one outcome of the new concept of cross-functional organization.

The traditional method, which consists in setting up each department of a company in its own watertight compartment, has the effect of dividing corporations into independent profit centres whose interests sometimes diverge. Implicative marketing must be the pivot of a coordinated transition toward a common and overriding goal. A company cannot function without separate units devoted to procurement, quality assurance, design, production, advertising, and so forth; nor can it function without cooperating with its stakeholders, from suppliers to consumers; and of course, it must be unconditionally connected to CSR experts.

While many corporations have added new watertight compartments to their conventional layout, such as a CSR unit or an office for participatory innovation, it seems more practical to locate such departments at the core of a new integrated system: an implicative system that involves the entire organization.

Choosing implicative marketing means choosing responsibility as a principle of development and making it one's mission to fulfil it properly (see Figure 5.3). This entails choosing to open up the organization to exchange and cooperation. In addition, it means choosing to reconnect with the consumer based on new contracts, namely, the following:

- The contract pledging to respect people and their yearnings.
- The contract pledging to be modest and to challenge the status quo.
- The contract pledging to make an ecological and economic transition.

## Reflecting anew on the products and services to produce: a *sine qua non* for engaging in implicative marketing

When people become insensitive to the hard-sell advertising of products and services, they devise other solutions to circumvent conventional implicatives. Moreover, these new solutions have multiplied and are more economical and in many ways more satisfying. No price can be placed on self-direction, freedom, social bonding, and esteem for durable products.

If corporations devoted just a little more attention to such new experiences, they would find in them several potential new products that could interest consumers, if suitably conceived to fulfil their desires. The consumption of organic food has grown fourfold in the ten years from 2005 to 2015 and fair consumption has been growing by 20 per cent per year since

*Figure 5.3* The three contracts of implicative marketing

2015. However, these are often expensive, which proves that emancipated consumers are capable of making sacrifices to fulfil their ideals. These are choices that demand personal involvement. They are implicative choices. QED.

By putting products and services on the market that fulfil these new expectations and by facilitating access to these new methods of exchange, businesses should be able to restore the consumer bond, regain consumer trust, and commit to a constructive economy. Let us review in the following some products and services that have emotional appeal to people, that is, users, consumers, and those whose purchases are not meant for final consumption.

### Products and services that are responsible, fair, and justified

Eco-design, fair trade, and organic food are new solutions to verified needs. They make acts of consumption meaningful, improve the quality of life of both their consumers and producers, and create a vision for the future.

#### Bébé Confort: Natural Comfort feeding bottle[3]

The issue: in a highly competitive market shaken to the core by the bisphenol A crisis, it occurred to Bébé Confort to create an alternative to the traditional glass feeding bottle for infants.

The solution: Bébé Confort conducted a comprehensive eco-design review of its baby bottle business and designed a bottle that fully satisfies the contemporary expectations of young parents concerning product safety and convenience. Bébé Confort's new feeding bottle uses 20 per cent less plastic, the raw material for its cardboard boxes comes from sustainably managed forests, and its bottle manufacturing was relocated to Europe. Most importantly, the new process will be reproduced for all the brand's future products.

#### Malongo: top-notch coffee thanks to full control of the supply chain[4]

The issue: In an ultra-competitive market for a mass consumption good, Malongo is the leading company that both sells organic coffee and practices fair trade. Motivated by its commitment, Malongo re-examined its supply chain from end to end.

The solution: In addition to selling a range of coffee varieties roasted the traditional way, Malongo designed recyclable pods for its coffee that are made from vegetable fibres and can be inserted in a matching, ecode-signed espresso machine made in France, resulting in reduced energy consumption.

## *Jimmy Fairly: the proper balance between the design-price ratio and solidarity*[5]

The issue: in a very competitive eyeglasses market, the selection is huge and the price range has lost all meaning, given free eyeglasses with extravagant designer frames, hard to discern quality, little information on where they were made, how long they last, useful life, so on and so forth.

The solution: Jimmy Fairly decided on a succinct product line with an ingenious contemporary design. The frames are handmade in Italy. The eyeglasses are offered in two qualities. The price range is very simple and reasonable. For every pair of glasses purchased, the consumer can give a free pair to somebody in France or abroad who needs them, under the solidarity motto "Buy one, give one".

## *Fairphone: reconciling digital and sustainability*[6]

The issue: the multiplication of digital tools has escalated the destructive impact of the electronics industry: increasing waste production, resource depletion, and perpetuation of social injustices.

The solution: responsible procurement, scalable equipment, user awareness: the entire company is mobilizing to offer equipment that focuses on reparability and to respect the workers who make manufacturing possible and the consumers who will use it. The design is modular and reparative, the batteries are replaceable and long-lasting. Furthermore, Fairphone is the first mobile phone brand to integrate fair trade gold into its supply chain.

## *Galeries Lafayette: a distributor takes its sector with it*[7]

The issue: we now know that the social and environmental impact of the fashion sector exceeds that of air transport and the automobile combined. Driven by fast fashion, this sector has recently become aware of its responsibilities and more sustainable solutions are finally being developed.

The solution: by launching *Go for good* in 2018, Galeries Lafayette chose to label all brands in stores that meet certain criteria, such as the use of organic cotton, the use of recycled materials or sustainable washing processes. With the commitment to have, by 2024, more than 25 per cent of the proposed offer labelled *Go for Good* and resale or recycling solutions for all products purchased in stores....

### From a new business model to new uses

How is a product made? How is it destroyed? For how long can it be used? What is its use-to-cost ratio? Has its useful life been optimized? Given an analysis of the flow of expenses incurred by a company and users, the consumption of energy and raw materials, and the actual use to which the product is put, a great amount of effort seems to be wasted. An automobile, for instance, spends more than half its life sitting in a garage while its owner is still paying off the car loan.

The principle of a functional economy consists in analysing the logic of both the manufacturing and the consumption process to design new arrangements, whereby what is bought and paid for is the actual use of the merchandise and the services associated therewith. This new way of thinking about how products are supplied and paid for would allow the user to buy exactly what the user needs and enable the seller to optimize its industrial process. This system would sharply reduce pollution and waste while releasing purchasing power to buy new and innovative supplies of products and services.

*RecyGo: a new company created by the French post office and the Suez utilities multinational[8]*

The issue: every day French mail carriers go to companies to deliver mail and then leave empty-handed. These same companies, especially the smallest ones, have trouble sorting their used paper.

The solution: the business should collect waste paper in a dedicated container provided by the post office. Mail carriers would then pick up the waste paper every day. Sorting would be done by a company that helps the long-term unemployed rejoin the workforce.

The outcome: the mail carrier's time is optimized, the company's paper sorting works smoothly and effectively, the paper is recycled in France, and the long-term unemployed are assisted in rejoining the workforce.

*Mud Jeans[9]*

The issue: not everyone can afford ecodesigned jeans, that is, jeans made from organic, recycled cotton in No Sweat workshops. Additionally, discarded jeans are seldom recycled.

The solution: anyone can afford healthy and durable jeans. How? Instead of buying jeans, you lease them from Mud for a small monthly fee. After 12 months, either you keep the trousers or you return them for recycling and you can lease a new pair.

The outcome: a total of 3,000 renters all over the World have adopted this new way of wearing their favourite garment (already millions of gallons of water have been saved) and share their vision of the circular economy. Mud Jeans' goal is to recruit one million followers.

### Michelin Fleet Solutions[10]

The issue: Michelin sells its tyres to haulage fleets, which are then in charge of maintaining them. Tyres are a big-ticket item for overland shipping companies and a sunk cost, even when tractor-trailers stand idle. If tyres are poorly maintained or underinflated, the truck's fuel consumption increases, along with its running costs and its environmental impact.

The solution: outsource the handling of tyres to the manufacturer that supplies them. Michelin supplies perfectly matched and well-maintained tyres to fleets that pay only for actual optimized use.

The upshot: optimized tyre handling for buyers, optimized service for Michelin, whose reputation flourishes as a result, and Michelin gains customer loyalty to boot.

### L'Atelier Bocage[11]

The issue: footwear is a particularly difficult product to conceptualize in terms of eco-design but also in terms of impact. Indeed, its various materials are firmly linked to each other and make it difficult to dismantle for recycling.

The solution: L'Atelier Bocage offers access to a shoe offer, for the price of a monthly subscription. After two months of use, the consumer can return the pair of shoes to get a new pair. The first pair is locally reprocessed at the factory and then rented on a second-hand site. Once worn-out, they will be recovered by the factory, which will control their destruction.

## Implicative advertising, so that advertising can finally become a joining of forces

Implicative advertising faces many challenges of both substance and form, including creating bonds, locating the right points of contact, fostering co-production, respecting its public, and sincerely conveying constructive messages. Speaking about implicative advertising might even be redundant. However, it is not just about communicating: it is about joining forces and about both sides making a commitment.

Conveying a responsible message and actually behaving responsibly oneself are not, however, the same thing! We are entitled to expect both of advertising. Advertising cannot be aloof from the message it conveys, because the medium and the message are inseparable. Although, as we have seen, not everything depends on advertising, starting with the subject to whose welfare it is devoted, this does not exempt it from ethics. We must not forget a fundamental precept: advertising means to make a commitment – "I do what I say and I say what I do" or "Talk the talk and walk the walk".

The very purpose of implicative advertising is to create bonds among people. Its responsibility is to do so while respecting both companies who pay for advertising and their public. It is not by accident but, rather, by design that I do not write here of advertisers and their targets. That jargon is, by definition, outdated and counterproductive. Viewing the public as a target entails placing it at a distance, to transmit a message more effectively. But that is exactly what we are trying to avoid. The new technical skills that advertising now has at its disposal to create conversation should enable it to develop a new role in an exchange and as a mediator between both parties concerned, namely, the company and its advertising audience.

Lastly, to find a fair place that is worthy of respect, advertising must combine its new tools with moral and social commitment. Implicative advertising can be summarized in the following five maxims:

## 1. Implicative advertising is immediate and sustainable

Implicative advertising must be attached to the immediacy of the exchange as well as to the lifetime of the relationship that has been or will be constructed. This double-track timeline is problematic. It requires a structure that is capable of responding but first, it must be based on a clearly defined structural vision, that is, a backbone that will enable sustainable commitment and bind the entire organization together to enable it to communicate consistently in various modes, on social media, when addressing the media and other items bearing its brand.

## 2. Implicative advertising is a conversation

Accordingly, implicative advertising must have a twofold structure, depending on both the market research tools used and the specific content and structures through which marketers address their audience. From this interactivity, a dialogue will be born that is essential for a robust relationship.

### 3. Implicative advertising is obviously sincere

To instil trust, implicative advertising must substantively respect its public by basing itself on proven facts and genuine commitment. Every item of information transmitted must be openly acknowledged and capable of being defended by every member of the company and all those with whom it does business.

### 4. Implicative advertising is attractive

Implicative advertising must elicit approval. Dialogue can only persist if it is pleasant and interesting. Consequently, implicative advertising's attributes contribute to its success. I readily admit that implicative advertising can be creative, clever, aesthetic, and funny and, contrary to popular belief, honesty and enjoyment are perfectly compatible!

### 5. Implicative advertising advances steadily

Implicative advertising is a construction, or a permanent reconstruction, based on a permanent ability to question the *status quo*. However, we must avoid being a weathervane, that is, always sharing the opinion of the last person with whom we spoke. The weathervane syndrome occurs most often in surroundings characterized by immediacy and unfettered speech. Actually, an ability to question the status quo goes hand in hand with constant reflection on past discussions. By definition, dialogue opens one's mind to opinions, praise, and reproaches. Implicative advertising should welcome this enrichment. Processing and assimilating this enrichment enables implicative advertising to continue advancing (Figure 5.4).

### 6   The elements of implicative marketing

Implicative marketing means forgetting about outdated reactions. To go beyond the traditional four Ps, we should add new axes perpendicular to the principal axis that will incorporate such aspects as retailing, advertising, and the attributes and price of the merchandise but, once again, from a new, seamless perspective. The following are the four axes that guide all efforts: supplying, supporting, committing oneself, and connecting.

### 1. Supplying

It is of course important for a company to provide satisfactory solutions to its consumers, but it is additionally important to provide pleasant and

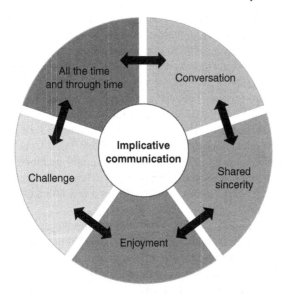

*Figure 5.4* Implicative advertising.

soothing products and services that are generally respectful of individuals and their environment. Innovative, co-created, attractive products and services must satisfy in terms of their use, their affordability, and the pleasure they give their users.[12] Such products and services can be inspired by traditional ones but if they are, they must be stripped of current flaws: they must be devoid of toxic substances and endangered natural resources. The output must be generated by clean and socially responsible production methods.

Many experiments are in progress and already leading to genuine advances. For example, Ecosia, the German search engine, is the result of its creator's search for an economic model with a positive social impact. Wishing to get involved in forest conservation to protect the environment, the idea of developing a research engine that would make it possible to finance planting and rehabilitation projects came to him. Ecosia.org was born in 2009.

Also, operating in the forestry sphere, Klorane controls the entire supply chain for its desert date palm shampoo, while encouraging reforestation and employment in Senegal.[13] In terms of supply chain engineering, the Serge Ferrari company, which manufactures composite materials used in construction and design, has devised a complete recycling system for its own needs. This segment of the company's business is now fully operational under the name Texyloop and shares its technology with other European companies in the same line of business.[14]

Such innovative solutions are sometimes prompted by demands expressly made of the companies concerned and some have already been market tested but remain inaccessible to consumers, for instance, second-hand merchandise in new sectors that is sold under warranty. Other instances are companies such as Etsy,[15] which match the supply and demand for products and services between consumers through online platforms, and platforms such as La Louve cooperative,[16] which facilitates cooperation between different businesses in the food industry. La Louve copied the business model pioneered by the Park Slope Food Coop[17] in Brooklyn, which was set up in 1973 and now has 16,000 members. La Louve operates a supermarket in the north of Paris where each member can buy quality products at low prices in exchange for a few hours of work at the coop every month.

In addition, such solutions must offer new opportunities emerging from technological or organizational innovation, such as recycled products. Up-cycling, a technique that is as yet scarcely explored, can become a line of work, or even a line of business, as it has become for Bilum,[18] which sells bags and decorations made from waste materials. Takari Design[19] is another example. Takari's recycling business helps sustain France's outlying possession of French Guiana in South America, where it turns wood from freight pallets and old fishing trawlers into design furniture for schools and public spaces. Eco-design, digital creation, and the development of Fab Labs has opened up new opportunities for waste recovery and the circular economy. These endeavours are encouraged by national governments. The French energy planning agency ADEME, for example, often calls for bids on its recycling projects.[20]

## 2. Supporting

The adoption of new consumption patterns must be facilitated: through guiding, supporting, and, most importantly, listening. Once a company has grasped the individual consumer's values and has redesigned its products or services accordingly, it must support the consumer without fail in building a new consumption processing scheme. More precisely, it must help consumers regain trust in a processing scheme that has been impaired by new constraints and new opportunities emerging in the consumers' environment.

Can we believe in a label? How does a supply chain's commitment change when it manufactures a food product? What is so wonderful about consuming French-made products? The answers will largely depend on information and the production of new knowledge that is sound, legitimate, and attractive enough to change the three levels of attitude: the cognitive, that is, what we know, where what we know grows; the emotional, that is, what we like, regardless of whether we are fond of it or not; and the conative, that is, what makes us act.

Thus, digital applications in the fields of cosmetics, food, and now fashion, such as Yuka or Clear Fashion, show that public demand is being responded to. Yuka has gathered more than ten million registered users in five years, including nearly three million active users. Scanning your products in the store to find out what they contain and where they come from has become a habit that requires manufacturers and distributors to review their assortment of ingredients and remove the controversial ones.[21]

Information allows the construction of a new knowledge base that enables new consumer experiences, because a bevy of new experiences requires effort and personal commitment and challenges one's beliefs and behaviour. It is difficult to change one's conduct to match this incipient attitude, especially in the context of buying staple products whose purchase has long been guided by habit and conditioned reflexes.

### 3. Committing oneself

Implicative marketing, as we have seen, is a kind of marketing that involves the relationship among its participants. Consequently, at this point, we must specify which sort of cooperative organization best suits the intended purpose, beginning with internal cooperation.

Workers should be hired so they can contribute to specific projects, instead of following the convention of assigning them tasks enclosed within silos. The efforts of design, research, sourcing, marketing, and advertising must take place in a coordinated fashion to manage the brand and keep it consistent.

These new project teams must incorporate new participants or, better yet, they should outsource individual tasks to contractors. The consumer has pride of place and must hold centre stage instead of continuing to play the subordinate role of experimental lab rat. Consumers must cease being merely the final link in the product testing chain or an isolated source of fresh ideas.

We must also, however, incorporate other stakeholders in the supply chain, that is, all the professionals capable of sharing their experience and asserting their needs: the installer, the procurement specialist, freelance consultants who work for the company from time to time, design and architecture firms, advertising consultants, and energy conservation and industrial property firms. All should join forces for the common good.

Consequently, companies must be restructured to enable cross-functionality without, however, overriding the specific expertise of individual departments. Cooperation will be motivated by awareness of shared interests. The company will benefit by adapting and improving its business performance. Its suppliers, subcontractors, service providers, banks, institutions, and so on, will benefit by being able to support and advise the company more effectively and the consumer will benefit from an increase in consumer utility.

Such a project requires structure and leadership such as those of creative communities, trading platforms, and beta testers. Internet industries and websites devoted to music and games already use these nimble models developed by start-ups. They drive the development of such models and offer new solutions. New structures offer mediation skills for developing innovative practices.

*4. Connecting*

Implicative marketing must lay the greatest emphasis on incorporating advertising into its model. Advertising must be integrated into the project from the start. Advertising will no longer be the final stage of a cycle. Instead, it must be the backbone of a comprehensive and continuous process of putting individuals in touch with each other. Advertising must encourage a reciprocal relationship that is freely entered into and constantly renegotiated.

Accordingly, to build a durable brand, advertising must pay attention and strive to understand the consumer. It must replace its one-size-fits-all communication technique with a complex model incorporating monitoring, listening, mediation, encouragement, announcements, and conversation. Its new media and the paid-owned-earned model[22] will facilitate these tasks. Advertising must produce meaning, which should, moreover, be useful, interesting, and appealing. Its boundaries are shifting. Just like brands, advertising has ceased to be the endpoint mouthpiece, clamorous but incoherent, of conventional marketing. It must now become the breeding ground of implicative marketing. It is obvious that its primary guidelines must be a non-negotiable policy of sincerity and honesty.

## Conclusion

Neither Roland Barthes' semiological scrutiny,[23] nor the American boycott movements of the 1960s,[24] nor the pacifist movement of Larzac in the 1970s and not even the first petroleum crises of 1973 and 1979 have managed to halt the marketing juggernaut, which still forges ahead, oblivious of history. The marketing apparatus dissects the consumers into oblivion, tearing them asunder amid economic hardship, artificially exacerbated cravings, guilt at environmental devastation, and fear of disease.

Today, however, marketing has exhausted its ability to impose a consumption model that ostensibly creates comfort and wealth.

### The consumer has changed beyond recognition. And it's catching!

In the course of half a century of consumer society, the individual consumer has constantly changed, if not transformed him- or herself. The most recent developments in this area show us that consumers are becoming increasingly independent. Considering themselves emancipated from the traditional economic system, they expect that their consumption will not harm themselves or others from an economic, social, and environmental standpoint. And nobody can object to such a trend. We are ready to learn and to engage in new experiences.

Although it has been confirmed that a genuine need exists for personal fulfilment through consumption, nowadays individuality is also expressed – perhaps paradoxically – within a social group or a cluster of social groups, namely, tribes. We still function with regard to others but we also act in common with them.

This commonality opens up new paths. This is because our consumer behaviour sends far more signals revealing our character than formerly and propagates new behaviour patterns. The evidence for this claim is that the places we select to perform our acts of consumption reflect our social status, what we do, or how committed we are. This effort can be made in common with one's family and friends, or cooperation can be extended instead to organizing one's coworkers in support of an association to preserve family farms or to get together with neighbours to invest in gardening equipment. In some such joint endeavours, we create bonds with strangers at the other end of the World to swap apartments, for example. The social group then becomes a rhizome, a horizontal root that sprouts fresh shoots every few inches and whose nodules stockpile energy. And that is just the beginning. Every emancipated consumer announces his or her experiences to those around and contributes to a collective learning process.

### The transition will forge ahead, under the following conditions

In recent years, uncertainty, loss of trust, ethical issues, and the first signs of consumer activism have gradually shifted power from the marketing industry to the consumer. Meanwhile, the economic crisis has reinforced this challenge to the status quo by helping alter the social role of consumption and discredit obsolete models and beliefs. We have reviewed our criteria in terms of quality, satisfaction, and trust. Finally, the experience of being permanently connected to online information and purchasing opportunities has changed our criteria for judging retailers and authority, while suggesting that alternative paths are possible. We now know that, today, many solutions exist to satisfy our needs that put the individual in the driver's seat of a system that treated the consumer for too long like an infant devoid of the ability to make decisions.

The coming years portend an emancipated consumer, open to new ideas, who awaits new paths and new projects. An opportunity for the company? Yes, because it is perfectly possible to build together with the company while bearing the new requirements in mind. Respecting each individual's autonomy, the meaning inherent in the products and services available on the market, and an effort in transparency will be absolutely essential to restoring trust. To achieve this, what is needed is to reconnect, rebuild healthy relationships, and really listen to the population's new expectations. Of course, it is indispensable to forsake the destructive logic of price wars and reconsider the assortment of available products and services, their value, and their consequences.

The new issues are before us. Brands will have to accept the uncertainty of a market in perpetual motion and the complexity that implies, and create new contracts with the public. They must urgently reassess the consistency of their contracts to supply added value bearing meaning, warranting an economic effort. Lastly, they must commit to supporting the efforts of their public and support the development of innovative ways of thinking and behaving.

In short, it is time for each brand to reawaken desire and persuade consumers that it is preferable to any other brand – with modesty and sincerity (see Figure 5.5).

| The vicious circle of Obsolete Marketing | The sustainability potential of Implicative Marketing |
|---|---|
| Promises of bliss | Helps you live |
| Authority | Proposal |
| Individual confronting the group | Individual within the group |
| Destruction | Sustainability |
| Seducer | Appealing |
| Reproductive | Creative soothing |

*Figure 5.5* From obsolete marketing to a marketing worthy of respect.

# Notes

1 A.H. Maslow, op. cit.
2 According to Schwartz, these values are concepts or beliefs that relate to desirable ends or behaviour patterns. They are not limited to specific situations and are the expression of motivations intended to attain specific goals such as security, achievement, and self-direction. They guide the individual's choices and allow the assessment of behaviour toward people and events. They are arranged by order of importance as guiding principles for life and reflect three universal needs: to satisfy individuals' biological needs, to enable social interaction, and to promote the group's proper functioning and survival. See *Les valeurs universelles de Shalom Schwartz* (1992), at http://valeurs.universelles.free.fr. See also www.lesmotivations.net/spip.php?article55.
3 See www.bebeconfort.com/fr-fr/allaitement-repas-soin/biberons-en-plastique-natural-comfort.aspx.
4 See www.malongo.com/valeurs/edito-edito.php?page=43.
5 See www.jimmyfairly.com/fr/buy-one-give-one.html.
6 www.fairphone.com/fr/.
7 www.galerieslafayette.com/c/go+for+good.
8 See www.recygo.fr/solutions.
9 See https://mudjeans.eu/why-lease-a-jeans.
10 See www.michelintruck.com/fr_CA/services-and-programs/michelin-fleet-solutions.
11 https://latelierbocage.fr/.
12 Sandrine Roudaut, "*L'utopie mode d'emploi*", *Expérimentation radicale*, Editions La mer salée, 2014, Rezé, pp. 143–233.
13 See www.laboratoires-klorane.fr/article/2/une-gamme-responsable.
14 See www.texyloop.com.
15 See www.etsy.com.
16 See http://dons.cooplalouve.fr.
17 See www.foodcoop.com and the Park Slope Food Coop video at www.youtube.com/watch?v= RwRG6stOIOI.
18 See www.bilum.fr/e-commerce/fr.
19 See https://takari-design.fr.
20 The French government's Investments for the Future Programme (*Programme d'investissements d'avenir*) is encouraging the development of a circular economy, focusing on three complementary areas: waste management, the reclamation of polluted sites and soil, and ecodesign. The programme funds technological innovations and innovative industrial solutions intended to increase the proportion of waste that is reused, recycled, and recovered, including energy generation. See www.gouvernement.fr/le-programme-d-investissements-d-avenir.
21 Le nouvel Obs, Morgane Bertrand, 2019-9-22 "92% des utilisateurs de Yuka reposent les produits mal notés" www.nouvelobs.com/economie/20190922. OBS18750/julie-chapon-92-des-utilisateurs-de-yuka-reposent-les-produits-mal-notes.html.
22 See the discussion on paid, owned, and earned media on p. 40, where paid concerns the space I buy in the media to spread my message, owned concerns the media that belong to me (website, Facebook page, branded app, etc.) and that I completely control, and earned involves all the places my brand is mentioned,

either spontaneously or prompted by an incentive from me (i.e., bloggers, Facebook, Twitter, and media relations are all earned).

23  R. Barthes, *Mythologies*, Jonathan Cape, 1972.
24  V. Bourgouin, "*Histoire de la protection du consommateur*", *Journal du net*, at www.journaldunet.com/management/expert/
33398/1-histoire-de-la-protection-du-consommateur.shtml.

# Afterword

As a teenager, I understood the meaning of feminism. Furthermore, I believed that feminism would soon outlive its usefulness. I became aware of racism and thought that it, too, was fated to disappear. And, of course, I discovered that the environment was swiftly deteriorating and I was certain that soon …

I am now over 50 years old and my conclusion is that all those struggles must still be waged. And I choose a positive way, I want to look on the bright side. I choose to see the glass as being half full of encouraging signs: a constructive economy is emerging, wasteful practices are in the process of being outlawed, and, most importantly as far as I am concerned, the educational system is incorporating these issues and relaying new concepts and prospects to French youth.

I am a professor of marketing. As recently as five years ago, I was the one making students receptive to sustainable development. Today, it is they who badger me about corporate responsibility and are committed to transforming their consumption patterns: "Professor, can we really believe what brands tell us about themselves? Do you think they really mean to keep their promises? Can you give us any pointers on getting a job with a company that is not just a bunch of rip-off artists?"

Yes, indeed. These young adults already routinely deal with issues of responsibility and sustainability in their daily lives. In the course of their studies, they likewise become aware of their future responsibility as professionals and of the awkward choices they must make in the short term. The facts are clear: they expect managers and businesses to fulfil their demands and their commitments, creating new shared intergenerational motivations.

Implicative marketing: my proposal for sustainable economy.

# Bibliography

## Books and articles

Alet C (2010) *La Société de Consommation en Continue*, Alternatives Economiques n°295, October 2010.

Aubert N (2003) *Le Culte de l'Urgence. La Société Malade du Temps*, Paris Flammarion.

Barthes R (1972), *Mythologies*, Berkeley, Jonathan Cape Ltd.

Baudrillard J (1998) *The Consumer Society: Myths and Structures*, London, Sage Publications.

Baudrillard J (2006) *The System of Objects*, London, Verso.

Bauman Z (2007) *Consuming Life*, London, Polity Press.

Bo D, Guével M, Lellouch R (2013) *Brand Culture*, Développer le potentiel culturel des marques, Paris, Dunod.

Bourdieu P (1984) *Distinction: A Social Critique of the Judgment of Taste*, Oxford, Routledge.

Charrel M (2019) "Les prix se tassent plus que le pensent les français", *Le Monde*, 19 August 2019.

Consales G, Fesseau M, Passeron V (1995), *La Consommation des Ménages*, INSEE.

Cova B (1995) *Au-delà du Marché. Quand le Lien Importe Plus que le Bien*, Paris, L'Harmattan.

Damgé M (2013) "Les français continuent d'aller à l'hypermarché mais ils n'aiment plus ça", *Le Monde*, 14 June 2013.

Dicker J (2012) *La Vérité sur l'Affaire Harry Quebert*, Paris, Editions de Falois, l'âge d'homme.

Dubuisson S (2009) *La Consommation Engagée*, Coll. Contester, Paris, Presse de Sciences-Po.

Dujarier M (2008) *Le Travail du Consommateur*, Paris, La Découverte.

Heilbrunn B (2010) *La Consommation et ses Sociologies*, Coll. *128*, Paris, Amand Collin.

Herpin N (2004) *Sociologie de la Consommation*, Coll. *Repères*, Paris, La Découverte.

Herpin N, Verger D (2008) *Consommation et Modes de Vie en France*, Paris, La Découverte, Collection Grands repères.

Hetzel P (1996) Les entreprises face aux nouvelles formes de consommation, *Revue Française de Gestion*, 110, pp. 70–82.

Hetzel P (2002) *Planète Conso: Marketing Expérientiel et Nouveaux Univers de Consommation*, Paris, Editions d'Organisation.

Huot A (2018) "Quelles marques gagnent la confiance des français?" *l'ADN*, 2 May 2018.

Iqbal N (2018) Generation Z: "We have more to do than drink and take drugs" *Guardian*, 21 July 2018 www.theguardian.com/society/2018/jul/21/generation-z-has-different-attitudes-says-a-new-report.

Kapferer J N (2005) *Ce qui va Changer les Marques*, Paris, Ed d'Organisation.

Kapferer J N (2013) *Réinventer les Marques*, Paris, Eyrolles.

Keller K, Fleck N, Fontaine I (2009) *Management Stratégique de la Marque*, Paris, Pearson Education.

Kerchkove S (2010) *La Dictature de l'Immédiateté*, Paris, Michel Y Editions.

Kotler P, Dubois B, Keller K, Manceau D (2012) *Marketing Management*, 14th edition, Paris, Pearson Education.

Ladwein R (2003) *Le Comportement du Consommateur et de l'Acheteur*, Paris, Economica.

Lambin J J, De Moerloose C (2012) *Marketing Stratégique et Opérationnel*, 8th edition, Paris, Dunod.

Lewi G, Lacœuilhe J (2016) *Branding Management*, Paris, Pearson Education.

Lipovetsky G (1983) *L'ère du Vide: Essais sur l'Individualisme Contemporain*, Paris, Gallimard.

Lipovetsky G (2003) *Le Bonheur Paradoxal, Essai sur la Société d'Hyper-consommation*, Paris, Gallimard.

Maslow A H (1943) A theory of human motivation, *Psychological Review*, 50, pp. 370–396.

Miller M B (1987) (trans. Jacques Chabert), *Au Bon Marché (1869–1920): le Consommateur apprivoisé*, Paris, Armand Colin.

Novel A S (2013) *La Vie Share*, Paris, Éditions Manifesto.

Pastore-Reiss E (2012) *Les 7 Clés du Marketing Durable*, Paris, Eyrolles.

Peytavin (J L) (1991) Années 90: la crise de la publicité. Fin de la poudre aux yeux, retour à l'authentique, In *Quaderni*. 1991–1992, La vulgarisation des Sciences Humaines.

Roudaut S (2014) *L'Utopie Mode d'Emploi*, Rezé, Éditions La mer salée.

Roudaut Y (2013) *La Nouvelle Controverse*, Rezé, Éditions La mer salée.

Sicard M C (2008) *Identité de Marque*, Paris, Eyrolles.

Sobczak A, Minvielle N (2011) *Responsabilité Globale*, Paris, Vuibert.

Touzé F (2014) Réinventer le marketing : comment re-séduire un consommateur émancipé, *Magazine des Grandes écoles*, 15, p. 19.

Touzé F (2016) Revendiquer son nom pour revendiquer ses actes, *La revue des marques*, 93, pp. 94–97.

## Online sources

### *Articles*

Bariet A (2013) "Comment cibler l'alter-consommateur", *L'Entreprise.com*, 27 March 2013, https://lentreprise.lexpress.fr/rh-management/marketing-comment-cibler-l-alterconsommateur_1523036.html.

Bertrand M (2019) "92% des utilisateurs de Yuka reposent les produits mal notés", *Le nouvel Obs*, 22 September 2019 www.nouvelobs.com/economie/20190922. OBS18750/julie-chapon-92-des-utilisateurs-de-yuka-reposent-les-produits-mal-notes.html.

Bourgouin V (2008) "Histoire de la protection du consommateur", *Journal du net*, 12 November 2008, www.journaldunet.com/management/expert/ 33398/l-histoire-de-la-protection-du-consommateur.shtml.

Charrel M (2019) "Les prix se tassent plus que le pensent les français", *Le Monde*, 19 August 2019.

Denoun M and Valadon G (2013) "Posséder ou partager?" *Le Monde diplomatique*, October 2013, www.monde-diplomatique.fr/2013/10/DENOUN/49720.

Di Grandé V (2013) "Face à la crise les francais se detournent de l'environnement", *Le Monde* 11 January 2013, www. lemonde.fr/planete/article/2013/01/11/face-a-la-crise-les-francais-se-detournent-de-l-environnement_1815651_3244. html#d6I90uhCq9QE0Ohl.99.

Durox S (2011) "Consommation: le nouveau statut de la liberté", *e-Marketing*, 1 March 2011, www.e-marketing.fr/Marketing-Magazine/Article/Consommation-le-nouveau-statut-de-la-Liberte-39114–1.htm.

Faure G (2015) "Génération Y... Les empêcheurs de travailler en rond", *Le Monde*, 14 April 2015, www.lemonde.fr/societe/article/2013/04/11/generation-y-les-empecheurs-de-travailler-en-rond_3158117_3224.html.

Huot A "Quelles marques gagnent la confiance des français?, *l'ADN*, 2 May 2018, www.ladn.eu/nouveaux-usages/etude-marketing/decathlon-michelin-leroy-merlin-quelles-marques-gagnent-la-confiance-des-francais.

Lavelle D (2019) "Move over millennials and Gen Z - here comes generation alpha", *Guardian*, 4 January 2019, www.theguardian.com/society/shortcuts/2019/jan/04/move-over-millennials-and-gen-z-here-comes-generation-alpha.

Nebia A (2012) "Les Français confirment leur désamour pour le commerce physique", *e-Marketing.fr*, 11 October 2012, www.e-marketing.fr/Thematique/retail-1095/Breves/Les-Fran-ais-confirment-leur-desamour-commerce-physique-195459.htm.

Newman D (2013) "The Role Of Paid, Owned And Earned Media In Your Marketing Strategy", Forbes, 3 December 2013, www.forbes.com/sites/danielnewman/2014/12/03/the-role-of-paid-owned-and-earned-media-in-your-marketing-strategy/#23379b0d28bf.

Papanicola M "L'insight consommateur, cet illustre inconnu", Les Echos, 30 November 2011, http://archives.lesechos.fr/archives/cercle/2011/11/30/cercle_40636.htm.

Prudhomme C (2013) "La fin de l'expansion effrénée des drives", *Le Monde* 3 July 2013, www.lemonde.fr/economie/article/2013/07/29/la-fin-de-l-expansion-effrenee-des-drives_3454863_3234.html.

Schwartz S "Les valeurs de base de la personne", *Revue française de sociologie*, 2006/4 vol47, www.lesmotivations.net/spip.php?article55.

Touzé F, Monnier H, (September 2015) "Finie la mercatique de papa: et si on passait au marketing implicatif?" *Brandnewsblog*, https://brandnewsblog.com/2015/09/20/lheure-du-marketing-implicatif-a-t-elle-enfin-sonne/.

Vega de la X (March, April, May 2011). "Consommer: Comment la consommation a envahi nos vies", Sciences Humaines, Grands Dossiers, 22, www.sciences humaines.com/consommer-comment-la-consommation-a-envahi-nos-vies_fr_398.htm.

Wood Z "Unilever warns it will sell off brands that hurt the planet or society", *Guardian*, 25 July 2019, www.theguardian.com/business/2019/jul/25/unilever-warns-it-will-sell-off-brands-that-hurt-the-planet-or-society.

## *Other*

Arpp, www.arpp-pub.org.

Atelier bocage, https://latelierbocage.fr/.

Baromètre Greenflex, www.greenflex.com/offres/produits-consommation-responsables/marketing-responsable/barometre-consommation-responsable-2019/.

Bébéconfort.com, www.bebeconfort.com/international/feeding-care/bottlefeeding-teats.

Bilum, bilum.fr.

Citroën advertising, www.youtube.com/watch?v=WXbHb3YhBLA, www.youtube.com/watch?v=4QOB1uBboSQ and www.youtube.com/watch?v=i4N-kHnrvRg.

CREDOC, credoc.fr.

Danone advertising, www.youtube.com/watch?v=RPo47jpeftc.

Etsy, www.etsy.com/fr/about?ref=ftr.

European Commission https://ec.europa.eu/growth/industry/corporate-social-responsibility_en.

Faculté Audencia, https://faculte-recherche.audencia.com/cvs/cv/florence-touze/?no_cache=1&cHash=8ac82b9ffea6080c05546abea11a1833.

Fairphone, www.fairphone.com/en/.

France Inter, www.franceinter.fr/emissions/service-public/service-public-02-mai-2014.

The Free Dictionary, www.thefreedictionary.com/showrooming.

Galeries Lafayettes, https://goforgood.galerieslafayette.com/.

Greenpeace, www.greenpeace.org/france/fr/getinvolved/Zara and www.greenpeace.org/france/fr/campagnes/ Toxique/Toxic-Threads/Levis.

Harris interactive, https://harris-interactive.fr/newsfeeds/classement-netobserver-des-sites-preferes-des-internautes-francais-2/.

Jimmy Fairly, www.jimmyfairly.com/pages/notrepromesse.

Klorane, www.klorane.com/fr-fr/content/la-marque-klorane.

La Louve, http://dons.cooplalouve.fr.

Malongo, www.malongo.com/presentation/.

Maslow A http://maslow.com/.

Michelin, www.michelintruck.com/services-and-programs/michelin-fleet-solutions/.

Moati P, Obsoco, Lobsoco.com.

Mud Jeans, https://mudjeans.eu/.

Observatoire    Cetelem,    https://observatoirecetelem.com/les-zooms/enquete-23-
    responsabilite-et-ethique-dans-la-consommation/.

Optic 2000 advertising www.youtube.com/watch?v=T6Afza7FS24.

The Park Slope Food Coop Foodcoop, www.foodcoop.com.

The Park Slope Food Coop Foodcoop, www.youtube.com/watch?v= RwRG
    6stOIOI.

Prix Pinocchio, www.prix-pinocchio.org.

Prodimarques, prodimarques.com.

Recigo, www.recygo.fr/.

Renault advertising, www.youtube.com/watch?v=dXJFEPDYM9A.

Serge Ferrari – Texyloop, www.sergeferrari.com/fr-fr.

Sircome, sircome.fr.

Takari Design, https://takari-design.fr.

TNS/SOFRES, www.tns-sofres.com/sites/default/files/2013.10.17-pub.pdf.

Valeurs universelles de Shalom Schwartz (1992) http://valeurs.universelles.free.fr.

Union des marques, ww.uniondesmarques.fr.

WIPO, wipo.int.

# Index

Page numbers in **bold** denote tables, those in *italics* denote figures.

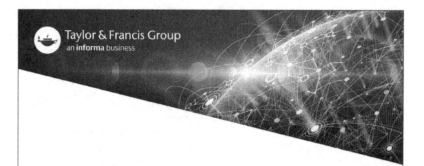